Hot Tips in
Sales Communication

Hot Tips in
Sales Communication

Bruce M. Arnold

To order additional copies of this book, contact:
Xlibris Corporation
1-888-795-4274
www.Xlibris.com
Orders@Xlibris.com
82175

CONTENTS

INTRODUCTION

Hot tips everyday are good. "Hot Tips" should be read while drinking your morning coffee, rich, fresh, and stimulating. This will get your business, sales preparations off to a great start. No matter what the weather looks like.

There is an old saying to remember about the September month: **"The important thing is not where you were or where you are, but where you want to get."** There is an every bit of human progress—our Inventions big or little, our type of business, our type of service rendered, and our business successes. We should first visualized before they became realities. Baby moons circle the earth not because of accidental discoveries, but because scientist set **"couquer space"** as a goal.

A goal is an objective, and as a purpose. A goal is more than a dream; it's a dream being acted upon. A goal is more than a hazy **"Oh, I wish I could**." A goal is a clear **"This is what I'm working toward."** No forward steps are taken until a goal is established. Without a goal or goals, an individual will just wander through life. An individual will stumble along, never knowing where they are going, so they never get anywhere.

Remember goals are essential to success as air is to life. So get a clear fix on where you want to go. Congratulations for a good September month, if you already plan your goals.

CHAPTER 1

GET THE NEWS YOU WANT AND THE CUSTOMERS "ARE" YOUR BUSINESS

The nation's leading advocate of expansionism and a formidable rhetorician on the subject, was a Senator in the 1800's, known as "*Senator Thomas Hart Benton of Missouri.*" His goal was known as the "*Prophet of Manifest Destiny.*" During his time, he had a good deal of help with his cause. The man who coined the phrase that brought the movement's goal, was a slogan from a New York City journalist named "*John L. O'Sullivan.*"

In July 1845, in an editorial calling for the annexation of Texas by the United States, O'Sullivan referred to the American people "*manifest destiny to overspread the continent allotted by Providence for the free development of our yearly multiplying millions.*" His message fell on ready ears. Expansionist sentiment was already widespread in the country and its partisans needed just such a sonorous "*Battle Cry as—Manifest Destiny.*"

In search for the excellence of the manifest destiny today, you must develop a formula to figure the true value of a customer and your goals. For example: Take the average purchase, and frequency, and calculate how much that customer could purchase in a year, if all purchases of this product or service were made by you. Then multiply it by to, for the value of that type of customer you wished to do business with. This represents the potential purchases over a decade, but doesn't even include referral business that customer gave you. Let's say a family might spend $150,000.00 for automobiles, for instance, using this formula. Isn't this customer worth spending time and money on your type of business and service?

Today, most businesses and successful salespeople devotes   much of their attention, time or money in keeping the customers. They spend tremendous amounts on advertising to attract new customers, but sometime lets the old one slip away faster than the new ones. This sometimes seems foolish way to spend money unnecessarily. Loosing that one old customer may set up back at least two steps in your goal. Remember the motto, "**Customers Are For Life**." This motto is made up with the "**Ten Commandments of Customer Service:**"

- *{1} **Bring 'em back alive.** Ask the customers what want and give it to them again and again.
- *{2} **Systems, not smiles**. Saying please and thank you doesn't ensure you'll do the job right the first time, and every time. Only systems **guarantee** you that.
- *{3} **Under-promise, over-deliver**. Customers expect you to keep your word. Exceed it.
- *{4} When the customer ask, the answer is always <u>yes</u>. **Period.**
- *{5} Salespeople, technicians and staff should be able to deal with customer's complaints.
- *{6} **No complaints?** Maybe good! But something's wrong. So, encourage your customers to tell you what is going on.
- *{7} **Measure everything.** Sports team do it. You should do it too.
- *{8} **Salaries are unfair.** So get trained with all and adapt, improvise, and overcome the objectives to a more profitable position.
- *{9} **Your mother was right.** Just like the boss would say, show the customer respect. Be polite. It works. And Finally—
- *{10} Learn how the best really do it. Make their system your own. Then improve your friendship with the customer.

And One For The Road—* **Stay in touch**! People resent feeling that they are only important until you sell them a service or a product, they are forgotten. There should always be at least as much effort, time and money expended towards building a long-term relationship with past customers as is spent on attracting new ones. This is considered an "**After-Marketing**," and can be done in many ways. *Newsletters, *Special sales for old customers, *Birthday Cards, and *The list is only as long as the limits of your imagination. Does if pay off? You bet it does, with referrals and repeated business. Customers will forgive mistakes and heartily recommend you to others. If they believe that you care.

CHAPTER 2

AN OLD INDIAN PROVERB OF
INTEGRITY AND GOAL SETTING

"Good morning, Grandpa Sun, Good Morning, I am so glad you came up today. Once again, you have brought light and the meaning into my life. Once again, I can feel the wonderful warmth of your face.

People say I worship you like a god. No, you are my friend and I talk to you like a friend. We both are a creation of our creator. Only you are much greater than I.

We each have a purpose for having been created. Yours is the light and warmth that you provide for all. Yours is for the energy needed for the growth of plants, creatures and goal setting. You tell us when we should work and do things.

My purpose is to enjoy life because of all that you give. I thank my creator through you. Your magnificence is something to behold. Without you there could not and would not be life.

This morning I have seen people about before dawn. Everyone busy going their own way. I wondered if they knew how good a feeling they could have if they stopped for a moment and looked up and said, **Good morning, Grandpa Sun, Good morning.**"

Someone once said that in looking for the right business and salesmanship within a company, one should look for **three qualities**:

*{1} Integrity,
*{2} Intelligence,
*{3} Energy.

If you don't have the first one, the other two would do the customer in. The cost for them, would be more than they wanted to spend. **Think about it; it's true.** If the customer still wants somebody without the first one, they really want them to be dumb and lazy. A good business owner wants his sales force, technicians and staff to have all three qualities when the business opens and leaves the business.

Research has shown **"Success In The Larger Sale,"** as an inconvenient way of coming up with the evidence that the researchers sometimes wish they'd never found. This sometimes occurred with the traditional theories of how to sell. This all starts out with our investigations on our classic sales-training methods that really worked and had a positive impact on sales success. The findings are challenge and perhaps the sales call consist of some simple and distinct steps:

* **Opening The Call**—The classic theories of selling teach that the most effective method for opening sales calls is to find ways to relate to the buyer's personal interest and to make initial benefit statements. This opening method may be effective in small sales but that they have a ambiguous success record in larger sales.

* **Investigating needs**—Almost everyone who's been through sales training in the couple of years has been taught about open and closed questions. These classic questioning methods may work in small sales, but they certainly won't help in the bigger ones. The more effective method of **investigating**, have been discovered from the analysis of successful sales calls and from the watching the **"Super Stars"** in action.

* **Giving benefits**—Once you have uncovered the needs, traditional sales training teaches you to give benefits that will show the features of the business and services that can be used to help the customer. Offering can be very successful in the small as well as the large sales.

* **Objection handling**—Overcoming the objections is a vital skill for sales success. The standard objection-handling techniques, such as clarifying the objection and rewording it in a way that benefits the close of the sale. These objection-handling skills are fine when you're making small sales, but in major sales, they can be very little effective. Concentrating on objection prevention, not a objection handling; is based on your analysis of how to do it.

* **Closing techniques**—The closing techniques that can be effective in smaller accounts will actually lose your business as the sales grow larger. Most of the commonly taught closing techniques just don't work for major sales. There are at least five known different types of closes that inter mix with the larger sales and they are:

> * **Assumptive Closes,**
> * **Alternative Closes,**
> * **Standing-Room Only Closes,**
> * **Last-Chance Closes, and Order-Blank Closes.**

In addition to the above **"Bread-and-Butter Techniques;"** there is what is known as the **"Classic or Exotic Closes."** They're known as the:

> * **Sharp Angle,**
> * **Ben Franklin,**
> * **Puppy Dog,**
> * **Colombo and finally,**
> * **Double-Reverse Whammo Close.**

No matter how hard you have tried to close, there is no reason to quit selling in this popular method of business and salesmanship. This a true way of measuring it by:

> * **Number of words written,**
> * **Number of instructural hours or,**
> * **Number of feet of training films endured.**

Using *Testimonials* as your closing technique, are quotations from satisfied customers and clients. This is one of the simplest and most effective ways of adding punch and power to the brochure, proposal, ad and direct-mail copy.

But how do you get *"Testimonials?"* How do you use them?

Here are some *Hot Tips* for using *testimonials:*

*1 *Always use real testimonials instead of made up ones.* When the most skilled copywriter can rarely make up a testimonials than can match the sincerity and credibility of genuine words of praise from a real customer or client.

If you ask a customer to give you a testimonial, and he or she says, **"Sure, just write something and I'll sign it."** Politely reply: **"Gee, I appreciate that, but would you mind just giving me your opinion of our service—in your own words?"** Fabricated or self-authored testimonials {those written by the advertiser or their copywriter} usually sounds phony. Genuine testimonials invariably have the ring of truth.

*2   **Prefer long testimonials to short ones.** Many advertisers are hooked on using very short testimonials. For example:
*   *... Fabulous !...*
*   *... Truly Ingenious ... thought—provoking ...*
*   *... Excellent ... wonderful ...*

Believe that when people see these **"Ultra-Short Testimonials,"** they suspect that a skillful editing job has masked a comment that was not as favorable as the writer makes it appear. The longer testimonials—say, two or three sentences versus a single word or phrase—come across, as more believable. For example:

"Frankly, I was nervous about using an outside service consultant. But your excellent service and advice has made me a believer! You can be sure that we'll be calling on your firm to organize all our major accounts for us. Thanks for a job well done!"

Sure, it's longer, but it somehow seems more sincere that a one word superlative which bring us to . . . .

*3   **Prefer specific**, detailed testimonials to general or superlative testimonials. Upon receiving a letter of praise from a customer, your initial reaction is to read the letter and find the single sentence that directly praises your company and or your salesmanship through the product and service. With a blue pencil, you can extract the words you think are kindest about the company, product, service and sales people. For an example: **"We are very pleased with your product and service."**

Actually, most of the testimonials would be stronger if you included more of the specific, detailed comments your clients has made about how your companies product or service help them. Address all, the prospects you are to sell to those who may have problems similar to the one current customer/client solved using the product or the service. If you let **Mr. or**

Mrs. Customer tell *Mr. or Mrs. Prospect* how you came to their rescue, they'll be helping you make the sale. For example:

"We have let you installed your new system/product for the service in each of your condominium/business complex buildings and have already experienced a 25 per cent savings in the management activity. Thanks to your system, we have now added an additional service with the decrease in management cost. This has increased profits 15 per cent and already paid back the investment in our association service. We are very pleased with your system/product."

Again, don't try to polish the customer's words so it sounds like professional ad copy. Testimonials are usually much more convincing when they are not edited for style.

*4   *Use Full Attribution*. We have all opened direct mail packages that contained testimonials from *"J.B. In Arizona"* or *"Jim S. Self-Made Millionaire."* Suspect that many people laugh at such testimonials and think they are phony.

To increase the believability for your testimonial, attribute each quotation. Include the person's are:

*(a) *name*
*(b) *city and state*
*(c) *their job title and company* (if a business customer) *e.g. *"Jim K. Redding, Vice President of manufacturing, Divemet Corporation, Denver, Colorado.*

Prospects are more likely to believe this sort of full disclosure than testimonials which seem to conceal the identity of the speaker.

*5   *Group Your Testimonials.* There are three basic ways to present testimonials:
     *(a) You can group them together in one area of your brochure, ad, or proposal.
     *(b) You can scatter them throughout the copy.
     *(c) A third alternative is to combine the two techniques, having many testimonials in a:
        *   *box*
        *   *buck slip*

> *   *smattering of other testimonials throughout*
> *the rest of the copy.*

All three approaches work well, and the success of the presentation depends, in part, on the skill of the writer and the specific nature of the piece. But, all else being equal, the first approach:

> *(a) *To group all your testimonials and present them as a single block of copy.*
>> *   *This can be done in a box,*
>> *   *on a separate page,*
>> *   *on a separate sheet.*
>
> *(b) *When the prospect reads a dozen or so testimonials, one right after another, they have more impact and power than when the testimonials are separated and scattered throughout the place.*

*6   ***Get Permission.*** Make sure you get permission from your customer/client to reprint his or her words before including his or her testimonials in your copy.

> *(a) *Suggest that you send a letter quoting the lines you want to reprint and ask permission to include them in ads, direct mail, brochures, and other materials used to promote your company's product or service.*
>
> *(b) *Ask for a general release that gives you permission to use the customer's quotation in all current and future promotions.* (not just a specific ad or letter)
>
> *(c) *This gets more mileage out of his or her favorable comment and eliminates the need to ask permission every time you want to use the quote in a new ad or letter.*
>
> *(d) *Whenever a customer/client sends a letter with a positive comment your service or products; immediately seek permission to use this testimonials in ad, brochures, direct mail, and other promotions.*
>
> *(e) *The easiest way to do this, is to send a "release letter" to the client (along with a photocopy of the*

testimonials letter, with the passages you want to reprint highlighted in yellow).
*(f) **Your release letter can follow this basic format:***

Mr. George Jones
Advertising Manager
World Enterprises
Anytown, USA

Dear George,

Thanks for your letter of 06/30/09 (copy attached). I'm glad you're pleased with **World Enterprises** service and products.

I'd like to quote from your letter in the ads, brochure, direct mail, and other promotions I/we to market our services and products—with your permission, of course.

If this is **OK** with you, would you please sign the bottom of this letter and send it back to me in the envelope enclosed.

The second copy is for your file.

Many thanks, George.
Regards,
John Smith

Yes, you have my permission to quote from the attached letter in ads, brochures, mail, and other promotions used to market your service and products.

Sign_____Date_____

When **"Goal Setting For Soliciting Testimonials,"** were seems as of moderate difficulty, people feel personally involved in your success. However, when goals were too stringent or lenient, only external evaluation is a concern with the **ABC'S** of conflict of resolution:

"A" greement and shared goals. Focus on these first, and keep coming back to them.

"B" ut, we'll have differences. Clarify them, value them, sort out those that you eliminate in various ways.

"C" ommit people to change.

"D" iagram the chronic cycle of sustained conflict. Have they been fighting together to avoid talking about important issues?

"E" xcel, personally. If others won't budge, what you do unilaterally?

Success in "Goal Setting," has been defined as a ***journey*** and not a ***destination***. However, without a destination, end results, or your goal to be achieved, there is no reason to start on any journey. If you are to be successful, ***you must first established the goals that are meaningful and worthy of your efforts.*** You must think in terms of end results, and then follow a plan to reach the desired goals. Your goals must become ***road maps*** to follow. When you begin the road trip across the country, you follow maps in choosing the routes, and you plan the trip with a day by day destinations.

When establishing a ***goal in life***, one must begin be achieving ***short term goals*** on your way to the larger ones. Before you can set a goal of any kind, you must determine what you have to work with, by ***APPRAISING YOUR PRESENT SITUATION***. As with the motor trip, one should need to appraise the car to determine if it is fit to make the trip. You take into consideration your finances, the first time involved, and various pieces of equipment you'll need for the journey. ***DO NOT START WITHOUT PREPARATION . . .***

Time must come to ***"Determine What You Want."*** You decide on a goal to be achieved and whether or not you are adequately prepared to make the ***journey.*** You decide what is to be accomplished when you reach the goals and why you want to reach that particular objective. This should give you the incentive everytime you wake up every morning to carry on. Just say, "***Thank God I'm Still Alive After Waking Up After Yesterdays Goal Setting.***"

Now comes the ***Development Of Your Plans***. As in the case of the motor trip, you spread out the maps and set out a day by day of progress to be made a particular time period. You set the timbale for achievement and then stay on schedule.

When the journey begins, you ***Convert Out Plans Into Action*** and follow through. It is here where most people stumble and fall. The best made plans are often thwarted because the maps for the journey didn't show detours, or you over estimated your ability to reach a particular destination at the particular time. For example, if your client doesn't send you a letter of praise, then you can ask them to give you a ***"Testimonial Goal"*** How you may ask? Simply send a to clients and customers who are are happy with your business product and services, and ask for their comments.

If you solicit testimonials from your satisfied clients and customers, and you always get permission to use any unsolicited testimonials that people send you, you'll soon build a thick testimonial file. Because you have gotten people to give you a "***blanket release***" to use their comments any way you choose, you can use these testimonials in any or all of the marketing materials—from ads, and sales letter, to brochures.

One quick and easy way to use these testimonials is simply to type them up a single-spaced and reprint them on an *8 1/2 by 11 inch* sheet of paper. The headline should read:

    *   *"**What They say about XYZ Corporation Service And Product**"*

If you have a lot of testimonials, you can print on the reverse side or go to a second sheet. Don't forget to include your address and phone number at the bottom of the page. Use the testimonials sheets as a handout, as an additional enclosure in direct-mail packages, or as a supplement to your sales brochure.

Always give the sheet and duplicate of your full testimonial files to any ad, copywriter, or marketing consultant within your corporation. It will be tremendously helpful to them when they create ads, brochures, and direct mail packages for you and your company.

Try this letter to use:
Mr. Alex Smith
XYZ Corporation
Anytown, USA

Dear Sir:

I have a favor to ask of you.

I am in the process of putting together a bouchure of testimonials—a collection of comments about our services and products, from satisfied clients and customers like yourself.

Would you please take a few minutes of your time to give me your opinion of my consulting services? There's no need to dictate a letter—just jot your comments on the back of this

letter, sign below, and return to me in the enclosed envelope.
(The second copy is for your file)

I look forward to learning what you like about my service....
but I also welcome any suggestions or criticisms, too.

Many thanks, Alex
Regards,

You have my permission to quote from my comments,
and use these quotations in ads, brochures, mail, and other
promotions used to market your services.

Sign_____Date_____

Note that by asking for an "*Opinion*" instead of a testimonial, and
Alex was to give criticism as well as positive comments. In this way, you're
just asking for a favor, and getting information that will help service your
clients better in the future. Thus, not only one who profits, because both
do.

Inconclusion to this chapter: if you haven't yet begun capturing
your customers and prospects by name, address, phone number and by
designation of their buying interest, do it now! Once you have a customer
list, you can start working it regularly. You can make monthly mailing
and /or phone contacts to announce: **(a) *New Products,* (b) *Services,* (c)
Pricing, and (d) *Sales.***

If you have a good mailing list, mail it often. It doesn't take any great
writing ability to make a great offer. All it takes is a simple understanding
of what people want. They usually want a: **(a) *Promise of a desired result,*
and (b) *Benefit to them;*** That could be an: **(a) *Advantage,* (b) *Protection,*
(c) *saving,* and (d) *enjoyment or even prestige;*** What they want to be and
feel: **(a) *Special,* (b) *More Important,* and (c) *Favored.***

A good business person can accomplish for them when you address
them in a letter form, as well as in person; in a special, respectfully distinctive
way. For instance:

*   **"*Dear preferred Customer,*" or**
*   **"*Valued Friend.*"**

You may also maybe very effective to alert them in advance to a buying opportunity, or to give them expanded understanding, or information that they didn't previously posses. When you communicate with your customers, clients, or patients, make certain that the information you share helps improve or protect their situation, not yours.

If an offer has value, people will appreciate hearing from you. So if you take the time to put enormous value into each communication you have with your customers or clients, you cannot communicate too often.

CHAPTER 3

HELPING CUSTOMERS MAKE A
TOUGH DECISION IN LOOKING AT
THE SERVICE AND PRODUCTS

One early spring evening, I walked around an old Native American dance ground. The air smelled of freshly fallen rains. I could see why this place was chosen for an encampment, the beauty of twight was breathtaking.

As I sat on a log surrounding the dance area, my imagination, or something was happening around me. I began to hear voices speaking a Native American tongue. The soft sound of a drum beat was becoming clear.

I could now hear horses and shouts of greetings, children were running about and playing. The smell of smoke and cooking became very strong, the beat of the drum began to get louder. The camp crier began calling names to come to the dance area. One of the names called was my great grandpa. I stood up looking around wanting to see him.

Singing began with the beating of the drum. The singing and beating of the drum was getting louder, I could see dancers very proudly dancing. The drum and singing filled me with strength and joy. I wanted to dance to express my feelings and to my creator.

This night I did dance with my godparents, grandmas and grandpas, I felt the same joy and feelings of many generations of my families and their people surrounding them. I know the drum is truly the heart of all people who listen. As long as the drum beats there will always be people who will listen.

Suddenly, I was standing all alone in the darkness. Still the smell of smoke and cooking was strong. I could still sense the movement of people about me. As I left the dance ground, I turned and raised m arm in farewell. I thank you . . . . I truly enjoyed myself.

When communicating the proposal to the customer or client, like the Native American Indian does when dancing on the old grounds and listening to the sound of the drums beat; would be considered the stepping point in closing the sale and thanking the customer for the business.

Sometimes customers may ask you, "*Which one do you like the best?*" or "*How many do you think I'll need?*" Be careful when communicating how you answer the question! Avoid making purely personal (or profit-motivated) recommendations. Customers and clients may blame you if they have problems or you may lose your credibility if they don't agree with your suggestions.

The best way to answer an opinion-seeking question is to give an example of what has worked for other customers in simular situations. You might say: "*Well, this one is very popular business service equipment with small or large families businesses your size; because it's roomier and built to take a lot of useage.*"

If the question relates to a personal decision, help your customers sort out their own feelings by asking an a probing question like: "*Which do you think would be easiest for you to use, monthly, bi-monthly, or quarterly services?*" or "*How often will you be using our service?*" Customers will be thankful when you help them reach an informed decision on their own.

Before you can be clear to others, you have to know what you're trying to say. Can you express your main point in one sentence? *For Example:* **Between the exterior and interior of your home lies a <u>No-Man's land</u> inaccessible to professional building code inspectors.**

* **Pick one main theme.** Stick to one main theme and three major subpoints. Organize any details under these and make your "*Outline*" clear to the customer you're communicating with. Like the "*camp crier*" at the Indian ***Dance Ground***, who tries to inspire the tribe, one message repeated over and over creates a more effective way of vision than a more complex message.

* **State what you mean.** One problem in many communication efforts is that some salespeople don't or will not say what they really mean. Sometimes it's to be tactful or avoid rudeness. If you

want the customer to draw your conclusion on their own, work at asking good questions that lead them where you want to go.

* **Listen more.** The biggest problem with most conversations, is that customers don't listen too well. To make sure the customer is listening, ***paraphrase*** what you hear from others. Then add what you infer from what you say that may not be explicit. Sometimes this called "***emotional reflecting***."

When dealing with commercial businesses, the manager make their living making judgments. When a task is relatively easy, high levels of motivation help the accuracy of judgments. But when the judgment task is difficult, highly motivated managers may make less efective judgments. Don't let them make snap judgments in complex task under high pressure. Take your time to work through the complexity for better judgment.

In conclusion to this chapter, there are ***22 Rules For Successful Self-Promotion***.

*1. Never tell anyone that you are not busy and that you are looking for work. (Clients want to hire those who are successful, not those who are hungry.)

*2. Always put your name, address, and phone number on every piece of promotion, brochure, you produce or service. This makes it easy for potential new business to reach you.

*3. Write a book. It positions you as an expert.

*4. If you the time write a book, write an article.

*5. When you write that article, try to sell it to more than one publication, such as a business or service magazine, or newspaper. You can change the title and a few of the examples to tailor it to each publication's readers.

*6. Regularly mail reprints of your articles to your prospects and clients. Attached a note or short cover letter to personalize the mailing.

*7. Advertise your services in magazines aimed at advertising professionals. Try a variety of journals and different ads until you find which ads give the best results. Also, try a both classified and display formats. You may want to search your territory to see what associations are their for your notability.

*8. Use direct mail to generate new business leads. A successful mailing of only a hundreds letters can often yield five to 10 highly qualified new prospects.

*9. Create a package of literature describing your company services or products, background, fees, methods, clients, and so forth. Mail packages to the people who requested more information in response to your ads and mailings. Such a package is extremely useful in "Pre-Screening Leads."

*10. Some copywriters, such as the **_Paul Bringe_**, have had great success using self-published newsletters to promote their services. Newsletters help build recognition and establish credibility with a selective audience over an extended period of time.

*11. Don't skimp of letterhead, envelopes, and business cards. The letterhead design and paper quality can convey an image of class and success.

*12. Package your copy so that it looks expensive. Type on high-quality paper, mail flat, and protect copy with cardboard, tissues and so forth. You can charge more if the product is worth more.

*13. Use a word processor. It will allow you to produce flawless manuscript as well as dramatically increase your productivity. Try investing in a small lap top computer that can be motivated from your home to your office and some times available use within your vehicle.

*14. Offer to speak and give seminars before trade association and professional groups such as commercial business management, condominium homeowners, and management groups. Make sure potential clients will be among those in attendance.

*15. Teach a course in advertising, marketing or writing to your fellow team members at a branch, district, regional, breakfast meetings.

*16. **_Network_**. Don't be a recluse—be social. Attend meetings, seminars, luncheons. Volunteer to work on a committee. Become visible in the advertising community.

*17. **_Recycle Your Material_**. A lecture can become the basis for an article or series of articles. The articles can turn into a book, using your basic material over and over makes it possible to get broad exposure and still have time to devote to your copywriting business.

*18. **_Be Selective_**. Not every opportunity to speak, lecture, write or participate is worthwhile. Focus on those promotional activities which will give you the most return on your time and effort.

*19. Keep your name in front of clients and prospects with a "**_premium_**." Most will appreciate your thoughtfulness. And the right premium—one that is kept in the office for years—serves as a daily reminder of you and your product or services.

*20. ***Let people know about recent success***. If your latest place or piece of copy was a rousing success, (such as the monthly sales letter) get extra copies and send them to prospects and clients in similar fields. Include a cover note that says, "***Here's what I've done recently—let me do the same for YOU!***

*21. Save any letters of praise you received from clients and build a "***Kudos***" file. (honor, glory, acclaim) Selected quotations from these letters—or even selling power of your next as or mailing. (Be sure to get permission first before you quote someone in print)

*22. Keep written records of past promotions and their results, Only by measuring the success or failure of promotional experiments can we learn which promotions work for us and which will bomb.

CHAPTER 4

HABITS
PERSONAL QUALITIES COUNT AND
STEPS TO ACHIEVE EXCELLENCE IN SALES

A **_Habit_**, is an act acquired by experience and performance regularly and automatically. A **_Habit_**, includes mannerisms, such as moving the hands when talking; satisfying psychological cravings, such as smoking or overeating, and even characteristic reading preferences, such as that for "**_Shakespearean tragedies_**. Most psychologists are interested in habits because of their functions as a basic element of learning and also as problems to be treated when they prove disruptive to a person's well-being.

A consider **_habits_** as an expressions, of aggressive impulses. Repressed, these impulses find an outlet through the counterproductive discharges that comprise **_habits_**. In contrast, the **_American Psychologist and Learning theorist, Clark Hull_**, defined **_habit_** with great precision in terms of the laws of conditioning and reinforcement. A majority of contemporary psychologists view **_habits_** as learned or conditional behavior over which one has little voluntary control. Some theorist even consider more complex human activities, such as playing basketball or speaking to the public and selling a service, as a composed of "**_habit hierarchies_**."

Habits may begin as reactions to a major event, such as winning as award, and then continues on other occasions that reproduce certain cues or stimuli from the original event. A **_habit_** is influenced not only by elements that bring the behavior about, but also by rewards or punishments or defeats that follow the behavior. An action that is lavishly rewarded as soon as it is performed is well on its' way to becoming a **_habit_**, such as a **_Super Star_**

Salesperson or Company Reward, within the industry's clientele. Once a *habit* is firmly entrenched, it can be sustained by cues different from those that originally created it. It may not be rewarded so well or regularly, but indeed, the *habit* may become its' own reward. A *habit* is always within the "*Winner's Circle,*" *of the "Super Star's Rewards.*"

When "*Promising a lot—An Delivering More!*" Here are "*Ten Effective Ways, Seven Laws of Satisfaction, and Seven Steps To A Better Plan*" after sales services can ensure repeated business, referrals, and positive references:

*1.   Only promise what you can deliver.
*2.   Don't over-commit other departments just to get the sale.
*3.   Communicate with new customers regularly.
*4.   Keep in touch with inactive customers.
*5.   Ask your new client how they would like you to service them.
*6.   Don't quote ranges in dates, prices or other areas.
*7.   *Communicate The Commitment* made to your customers to other departments that are affected.
*8.   Conduct an *after-sales* audit of the process and the customer feelings, opinions, etc.
*9.   Write down promises and commitments made to them in a file somewhere. Remember where you put it—preferably with their file somewhere.
*10. Check with your customer to determine the level of performance of your company for their perspective.

Seven Laws Of Satisfaction:

*1.   Treat the customers you have as though they're prospects.
*2.   View the customers as your partners—as members of your team.
*3.   Consider recruitment as a serious business—and hire only the best prospects.
*4.   Give your fellow team members the tools they need to build skills and develop professionally. Evaluate them on what they accomplished with your management, not hours worked.
*5.   Prepare for the inevitable conflicts that arise in any customer relationship with this thought in mind: "*It's how you handle problems that sets one professional or companies apart.*"

*6. Invite customer complaints instead of just responding to what comes in.

*7. Foster exchanges among team members to get their ideas on how to better satisfy customers. Test what you assume is working—even in your best program.

Seven Steps To A Better Plan By It Crafting Clear And Simple:

*1. Describe the purpose of your marketing proposal.

*2. Clearly explain what customer benefit you'll stress.

*3. Define your target audience.

*4. List your key marketing techniques.

*5. Declare your **_marketplace niche_**—the position that you feel is your in the eyes of your customers and prospective customers.

*6. Describe your Identity—the way you see within your company.

*7. State your marketing budget (**_your bid_**) as a percentage of projected gross revenues.

The best motivators are not the people with the most talent, it is your **_Personal Qualities That Count More_**. Here are some of the most qualities that can help to make your **_Human Resources Department_** the best that it can be:

*1. **_Vision_**: A clear view of what to happen in your service or sales department and a plan for bidding it into reality.

*2. The ability to communicate, which means knowing how to deal with the other team members.

*3. **_Open-mindedness_**: A good motivator must admit mistakes and realize that someone else's ideas can have value.

*4. **_Empathy_**: You need to be concerned with both the team members and their jobs within the company system. People must know that while the work is important, you feel they are important, too.

*5. **_An outgoing personality_**: You have to like dealing with team members and jobs within the company system.

*6. **_Setting a good example_**: If you haven't stepped into the shoes of team members in your department, maybe it's time you do so.

*7. **_Giving team members a chance contribute_**: Contributing team members are productive and generally satisfied with their work.

AS a followed team member coach, supervisor and motivator, you can take the role of coach, encouraging your fellow team members to solve the problems and recognizing their efforts.

*8. ___Showing enthusiasm___: There are three stages to an incentive program:

   *[a] Seeing the need for one;

   *[b] Setting it up; and,

   *[c] Getting enthusiasm about it.

Solving problems are the acronym (meaning words forms with other words) ___PRESTO___ suggest an approach to the problem-solving and creativity.

*   ___Prepare___: Prepare by learning all the details of the problems.

*   ___RANDOMIZE___: Randomize by combing elements or intruducing new thoughts, like random words or metaphors. That stimulates you to brainstorm for possible solutions, including ridiculous ones (you can do this by yourself).

*   ___EVALUATE___: Once you have a lot of ideas, evaluate them.

*   ___SELECT___: Select the most valuable ideas.

*   ___TEST___: Test these ideas on other people, or in other inexpensive ways.

*   ___OPERATIONALIZE___: And finally, operationalize by implementing the new solution throughout the organization.

Recently, research confirms that team members "___Brainstorming Benefits___," alone are more productive than team members brainstorming in a group. Team members feel more productive in a team because they hear more total ideas. But, because only one team member can talk at a time, the number of ideas that can be expressed is limited.

Brainstorming is fun, and because the teams works together to generate ideas and modify them, a sense of commitment to the solutions eventually chosen is generated. If you want a higher quantity of ideas, have the team members free associate by themselves. If you want enjoyment and commitment to ideas, use "___Team Brainstorming___."

CHAPTER 5

IMAGINATION—SIMILE—WISDOM

Imagination, Simile, and Wisdom came from the "***Big Horn Mountain Men***," during the 1800's. These mountain men were a breed apart. They roamed the wilderness hunting and trapping beaver until 1840. Yet, during this time period, they explored and marked trails that later supported the opening and settlement of the American frontier.

During these "***shining times,***" over 3000 mountain men traveled the land west of the Mississippi River. Some mountain men trapped for fur companies such as the "***American Fur Company,***" and the "***Hudson Bay Company.***" Other mountain men called themselves "***Free Trappers***" and trapped independently.

Mountain Men trapped their furs and beavers in the winter months when animal pelts were the thickest. Winter in the mountains was harsh and the mountain man often lived in total isolation. Many mountain of the men sought companionship with the Native American Indians. There was learning and adopting Native American lifestyle and techniques for survival. Come the spring and the thaw, the mountain men took their pelts and plews to "***Rendezvous***" to trade for much needed supplies. The meeting place had been mutually agreed upon the year before. Rendezvous was a time to rejoice, lie of course, "***palaver,***" gamble, compete with the black powder guns, rifles, tomahawks, and a knife. This renewed old friendships, and remember those who had "***gone under.***"

After the Rendezvous, the mountain men packed his plunder and disappeared once again into the mountains to become one with the wilderness.

Jedediah Strong Smith, (1798-1831) an American Fur Trapper and Explorer, born in Banibridge, New York. He became a fur trapper in the

West as a young man and in the last six years of his life, earned a place as one of the *"Greatest Pathfinders"* in

American history. In 1826, he ventured southwest with a party of 17 from the Great Salt Lake in search of trade routes, for fur trapping rights to California and the Northwest. After crossing the Mojave Desert, he reached Mission San Gabriel, California, near present day San Diego, and was probably the first white man to reach California from the East. Later on, he proceeded north to become the first American to cross the Sierra Nevada Mountains; proceeding across present day Nevada, he become the first white to pass through what now known as *"Reno"* and crosses the Great Salt Lake Desert.

With this all in mind, consider you as a *"Mountain Man Of Today."* You may not be trapping beavers, but going after the business and the service, you mean the same. Without meeting once per year to trade your pelts and plews, you would be and could be missing an annual *"Super Star Winners Circle,"* within your line of business. Their you will meet your friends and rejoice on what you have achieved. There maybe some competing but I assure you that you not used a black powder gun, hawk, and a knife to achieved or show your goals. Just trying golfing, fishing, riding horses and some conversing but most of all, you will be remembered as an *"Big Horn Mountain Person."*

Imagination, a conscious mental process of evoking ideas or images of objects, events, relations, attributes, or processes never before experienced or perceived. *Imagination, perception,* (the conscious integration of sensory impressions of external objects and events), and *memory* (the mental evocation of previous experience) are essentially similar mental processes. This is particularly true when their contents consists of sensory images. Psychologist occasionally distinguish between imagination that is passive or reproductive, by which mental images originally perceived by the senses are elicited, and imagination that is *active, constructive, or creative*, by which the mind produces images of event or objects that are either insecurely related or unrelated to the *past and present reality*. At one time your team *imagination* included the reviving of *"recollecting"* processes (memory), as well as the process of creating mental images (*imagination*). The present stricter definition of memory, as the concept of forming something new *contrast* with that of *reviving* something old.

There are *"6 Rules For Overcoming Objections:"*

*1. ***Don't argue.*** Never begin with "***no,***" *and* never say "***yes, but . . . ,***" That is another way to say "***no.***" Never used the word "***objection.***" Refer to it as a "***concern***" or *an **interesting point.***"

*2. ***Don't answer too quickly.*** Pause for a moment and reflect on what the customer said. If you jump in too quickly, he'll feel pressured.

*3. ***Don't over answer.*** Just answer it, don't bury it. Some team members attach too much meaning to an objection.

*4. ***Don't be drawn into pointless wrangles***. Not all objections can be answered satisfactorily. No product or service is perfect.

*5. ***Don't guess at an answer.*** If you don't know how to answer an objection, don't try. You'll lose credibility. Promise to find out and get back to the prospect.

*6. ***Be confident in your answer.*** If you doubt it, so will your prospect. Never ask, "***have I answered your objection***?" You're asking the prospect to admit he's wrong. He'll add another objection just to save face.

Simile, comparison by means of the words "***like***" or "***as***" between two kinds of ideas or objects. Examples of the ***simile*** are contained in the sentence "***Christianity shone like a beacon in the black night of paganism***" and in the line by English poet ***William Wordsworth: "But, like a thirsty wind, to roam about."*** By comparing ***Simile*** to ***Metaphor,*** which is use of a word or phrase denoting one kind of idea or objection place of another word or phrase for the purpose of suggesting a likeness between the two. Thus in the biblical ***Book of Psalms,*** the writer speaks of ***God's Law*** as a "***a light to his feet and a lamp to his path.***" Other instances of ***metaphor*** are contained in the sentences "***He uttered a volley of oaths***" and "***The man tore through the building.***" or "***This company has extended its' strength and wisdom to the customer who calls.***"

Figure of Speech, are words or group of words used to give particular emphasis to an ***idea*** and ***sentiment***. The special emphasis it typically accomplished by the user's conscious deviation from the strict literal sense of a word, or from the more commonly used form of word order or sentences construction. From ancient times to the present, such figurative locations have been extensively employed by writers to strengthen and embellish their styles of speech and composition.

A number scientist and thinkers were people who overthrew our inherited ideas about logic, language, learning, mathematics, economics and even space and time. Some were reflected on our times, the century. It was the age of splitting the atom and conquering sales, diseases, of probing our own psyche and the nature of the galaxies. It gave us the transistor and the silicon chip, plastics and artificial organs, televisions, chemicals, satellites, computers, new technology in industries and the atom bomb. What ever went on, we can still reflect back on the word *__Simile__*.

Activities For Team Thinking Creatively:

* *   *__Goals:__* To encourage the team members to think creatively as they respond to unusual questions.
* *   *__Materials:__* A copy of an *imagination list.*
* *   *__Sittings:__* An office, kitchen, business, an association meeting, or a house in which you can participant comformably with a prospect(s).
* *   *__Time:__* Five, ten, or even thirty minutes.

__Procedure:__ **1.** The team member asks the prospects or customers to let their minds expand in order to allow for innovative ways of thinking and perceiving better ways to eliminatetheir problems.

Next, the team member explains that this meeting the member will asked the prospects of customers to respond to some questions and then to explain why they respond as they did.

The team member at ramdom in a group meeting with the company or association will ask them from a *__Imagination list.__* When responding to the group, their response of which will be rationale can continue until each member of the company or association is satisfied and is willing to proceed.

The member initiates a processing discussion in terms of the activity's relevance to problem solving, brain-storming, or examination of basic assumptions.

*1.   What shape is a wish?
*2.   What does happiness look like when the service is compled?
*3.   What promotes a monthly or periodically follow ups on the product or service?

*4. What happens to your neighbors when you complete your service, when the garages are so close to each other?

*5. What does self-images sound like?

*6. What does a rainbow feel like?

*7. What is the time renewal option service like?

*8. What is your favorite sense?

*9. What does inspiration taste like?

*10. What is the weight of your anger?

*11. What is the shape of your imagination?

*12. What does your favorite referral book feel like?

*13. What does a cloud of inspiration sound like?

*14. And, What does the feeling to be a "**_Super Star_**" within your business Like?

When you add up an imagination, they soon become relativity.

When **_Optimists Succeed Where Others Fail_**, the **_Optimistic_** team members are successful because they persevere. In the face of temporary setbacks—and even complete failures—they persist. Everyone has their own point of discouragement; their "**_wall_**".

Optimism really pays off when the going gets tough. The critical juncture when the competition is also hitting "**_the wall_**" and ready to give up. The difference between **_success_** and **_failure_** is often that few extra inches it takes to get beyond the wall, and past where everyone else gives up. A little extra effort can pay off in big dividends. **_Failure_** does not stem from laziness, lack of talent, or lack of imagination.It's simply ignorance of some very important skills about the use of **_Optimism_**. **_Optimism_**—or to use an old phrase—"**_Positive Thinking_**" can make the difference between getting the job done well or not at all.

Low-Key Networking are prospects or customers, who are tired of having business cards pushed at them at social and networking events. Use your time to greet important prospects and customers you want to make sure to talk to; such as your boss or clients. Use the rest of the time to meet new prospects and learn about them socially. Talk about anything but work to begin to build the relationship. When you're not trying to sell, you—and they—will be more comfortable in these awkward situations. Remember, "**_Fools Rush In_**," so don't rush when trying to make a sale. If the customer ask a question, they may not be convinced by a brilliant answer. Think about what is really being asked before you overwhelm the customer with information. Give the prospect the time to develop the confidence in you.

Wisdom is generally pictured as a "*the quality or state of being wise. A scholarly knowledge or learning a wise act.*"

A group of frogs were traveling through the woods, and two of them fell into a deep pit. All of the other frogs gathered around the pit. When they saw how deep was, they told the two frogs that were as good as dead.

The frogs ignored the comments and tried to jump up out of the pit with all of their might. The other frogs kept telling them to stop, because they considered that they were all dead. Finally, one of the frogs took heed to what the other frogs were saying and gave up. He fell down and died. The other frog continued to jump as hard as he could. Once again, the crowd of frogs yelled at him to stop the pain and just die. He jumped even harder and finally made it out.

When he got out, the other frogs said, "*Did you not hear us?*" The frog explained to them that he was deaf. He thought they were encouraging the entire time.

This story teaches *two lessons*. There is power of life and death in the tongue. An *encouraging* word to someone who is down can lift them up and help make it through the day. A *destructive* word to someone who is down can be what it takes to *kill them*. Be careful of what you say. Speak life to those who cross your path. The power of words . . . . it is sometimes hard to understand that an *encouraging* of words can go a long way. so this day forward, think before you speak!

Wisdom Tales, is a demonstration of innate wisdom and good counsel in myth, folklore, and legends. It also a *Mentor* (mythology) in "*Greek*" mythology, where elderly friends and counselors of the hero "*Odysseus*" and tutor of his son, "*Telemachus.*" In the *Odyssey* of "*Homer*," the goddess of Athena, frequently assumes the form of mentor, when she appears to Odysseus and or Telemachus. English tutor's name has become an eponym for a wise, trustworthy sales person, teacher or counselor.

Reinforcing the Wisdom with your *Bosses* and *Team Members,* is someone who has the power, and doesn't mean that he or she doesn't need *encouragement*. Think about it, when was the last time you gave your boss or team member a hug? Not a *physical hug*, but a *psychological hug*. Thank them for their support or for doing a good job on a certain task.

Wisdom with our love for our kids doesn't depend on our kid's *achievements*. We love our children without any *contingencies*. It is what is called ***unconditional love***. The same approach is needed in the workplace today. We need to learn to trust and respect others even when we may at times have a problem with their behavior.

Wisdom can help everyone on the team and managers in the workforce feel good about themselves, we'll have team members and managers willing to ***share power***, permit others to take initiative and make decisions, and let team members and managers be the ***main vehicle for decision making***.

To overcome the ***"ego addition,"*** team members and managers have to get in touch with their ***own worthiness*** (upper management) If that is hard for them, others can help. The goal of everyone should be to ***maintain or enhance the self-esteem*** with whom you ***interact***.

CHAPTER 6

ATTITUDE
IN PROBLEM SOLVING

A known architect and writer **Charles Swindoll,** express his views on *"Attitude,"* as those who made it to the "*Winners Circle*" in the business or salesmanship. Those who did not make it, have a mountain to climb for the following years opportunity. His quote goes as follows:

"The longer I live, the more I realize the impact of attitude on life. Attitude, to me, is more important than facts. It is more important than failures, than successes, than what other people think or say or do. It is more important appearance, giftedness, or skill. It will make or break company . . . a [school] . . . a home. The remarkable thing is we have a choice every day regarding the attitude, we will embrace for that day. We cannot change our past . . . we cannot change the fact that people will act in a certain way. We cannot change the inevitable. The only thing we can do is play on the one thing we have, and that is our attitude . . . I am convinced that life is 10% what happens to me and 90% how I react to it."

When starting out every day, **problem solving is number 1** again in solving the customer's needs and desires. By following these four recommendations, you will get off to a running start for the "*Winners Circle.*"

*1. *Evaluate the possibilities.* Only after you have 20 possibilities you should try to weed them down to 5-8 realistic probabilities.
*2. *Refine solutions, then make an effort to improve each of the best possibilities.* Try not to rule out possible solutions too early.

*3.   *Choose a solution.* Pick the best solution available, even if your choice isn't ideal. Then try implementing it in a test way.

For example in the Pest Control Industry: Fumigation vs. Clean Heat vs. Local Treatments. In the Tire Industry: Goodyear vs. B.F. Goodrich vs. Firestone.

*   *Use the feedback.* No solution is likely to be perfect. Working with one solution gives you more information to go back and improve earlier stages like redefining the problem, or creating new possible solutions.

A growing number of companies who develop regions, are providing what is know "*Chaplins*," or better known as the "*Regional Sales and/or Service Managers.*" They provide to all, sales and service people and assistance programs. The ministers spend several hours per week at the branches or meet with you all outside the workplace, generally at a job bid site. If you feel that you and your manager could benefit from having a chaplin, priest, or rabbi with you all at a job bid site that you're proposing; then have your manager call for your local regional sales or service managers to discuss the possibilities.

Laughter can be the best medicine. Humor can be very effective tool for establishing rapport and setting prospects at ease. A good salesperson use humor during the warm-up phase of their presentations to set up a happy tone for the sales meeting.

But be careful when using humor. Observe your prospect for signs that certain types of humor may not be appreciated. Try determining the demeanor of each individual prospect before telling a joke. The wrong humor will kill the sale as quickly as the right humor will move it forward.

Whether you are in sales or service, and you donate time, money, or both, people who give themselves away agree that helping others makes them feel terrific. A study found that those who are active, lived longer, healthier lives than those who were not. The bottom line is, companies who are in the "*Winners Circle*," lived longer and succeed. Some scientist think that sales and service people, who volunteer, produces a "*Helper's High*" the exhilaration caused by the release of endorphins, then brain's own mood-elevating chemicals. Better known as the "*Winners Circle Companies.*" So, volunteer in your company, branch, district, or region, and not only will it help your sales, but it might make you healthier.

The practical approach to giving when within sales or service; the people giving money to charities, are better off targeting the charities that mean something to your sales and services. for instance, *"Mac Donald's Hamburgers"* spends around $2 million per year on social programs. You may not have to donate that much, but you will get some referrals from them. *Mac Donald's* use *five principles* to guide their giving and you can do the same.

*1. *The charities must be relevant to Mac Donald's business.* For instances, Mac Donald's supports "*Children Prevention,*" which make people feel safer to come out and eat at their hamburger facilities.

*2. *Have a target audience in mind for each donation.* Mac Donald's gives to groups that relate to their facilities, to opinion leaders in the community, most of all, to children (e.g., they support women's issues because two-thirds of their employees are women). Companies can give to the same groups, by contacting church's, businesses and to the community leaders who are elementary, and high schools and colleges, parks and recreation facilities.

*3. *Support a manageable number of charities instead of trying to cover the field.* Charities always have employees working for them, and generally own a home, a condominium, or an apartment facility. They will need your assistance, to help prevent nasty complaints about those unwanted events.

*4. *Build a leadership position for a particular cause so you will stand out in your target audience's mind.* By seeing employees and letting management know that you are their to help them and with their employees, will rotate your business cards for years. For example: Donate to charities, sports clubs, schools, and girls and boys scouting clubs, so that you display your banner and hand out your business cards.

*5. *Analyze how effective each potential recipient is in using money.* The more you explain what they are receiving and why you are estimating the cost of the service, they'll be more than likely refer you to other staff members and relatives about your business.

When you are sleeping and suddenly you wake up to figure out, "*How you were going to be successful this year* ?" Here are some ways that will make your tasks at work positive experience that challenges you at just the right amount of being on the top within "***Winners Circle of Your Industry.***"

*1. They're Short-Term.
*2. They're focused on a goal with clear results.
*3. They're a personal challenge.
*4. There's a sense of urgency.
*5. The task has a champion. There's clear leadership.
*6. **You don't get bogged down in routines. You skip the red tape.**
*7. You're committed.
*8. There's a pride of achievement.
*9. There's collaboration to succeed.
*10. This shows a "***Breakthrough of Strategy***," that can give more than one step into the "***Winners Circle Within Your Business.***"

Good sales or service people always needs something to be proud of when called upon and ask "***What the most interesting thing you do ?***" Most people don't have an answer. Many sales and service people haven't crystallized what your strengths and written them down. Many haven't communicated these strengths to management and customers. Both management and customers want to do business with their sales and service force who stand for something. If you're not excited about about something, you're at a big disadvantage in the latter part of the 90's and into the turn of the century.

More and more service technicians who been on the service side of the business are having a successful transfer into sales careers. Your points of view are the same as the buyer's because you have been with more directly for the buyers initial services. You've never been trained in all the traditional, nasty ways to trick the buyers into buying. You don't have to the adversarial attitude towards customers that some on the old-lines sales types do. You're on total product and customer service knowledge and a true interest in what the customers needs. You are also effective because the customers don't see interacting with them as sales calls, but as opportunities to get some free consulting and networking with a peer. For technicians, people skills, this is a good career transfer.

There are many things you can measure in sales. Putting clear numbers on them, it's easier to hold people to productivity schedules. For instance, number of calls per person, number of sales closed per call or proposal presentation, number of new accounts per month or bi-monthly. Support salespeople in the efforts that your managers are measuring.

In a recent study, salespeople greatly over estimate the quality of the relationship you have with customers. The conclusion drawn from a study in which **173 managers**, who received from **193 sales representatives,** who sold service and both groups also rated the quality of the sales person per customer relationship.

The art of selling isn't a matter of knowing what to do, but of doing what you know. Are you doing the following?

*1. ***Selling benefits, not features.*** Tell everyone what's in it for them.

*2. ***Using testimonials.*** Ask every satisfied customer for a written testimonial? Use them to offer proof of your claims to skeptical prospects.

*3. ***Delivering on all promises*** ? There are a few things that can damage a sales person's reputation faster than failing to keep your word.

*4. ***Speaking in public, commercial prospects*** ? Become known as your area's ___expert___.

*5. ***Getting lucky*** ? **Realize that the harder you** *work*, the *luckier* you get.

*6. ***Networking, Networking, Networking?***

*7. ***Using time wisely*** ? Take ***advantage*** of every second.
    It's the one commodity we can't buy more of.

*8. ***Digging for the real objection*** ? Most customers won't tell you the ___truth___ the first time around.

Don't plant doubts in your prospects mind, as it is good to anticipate and answer ___objections___ before they arise. Don't load your presentation with prospect with arguments that might sound defensive. Some salespeople, in an effort to head of objections, end up putting the objections into the buyer's mind in the first place. Some say things like:

*1. The price is amazingly reasonable—considering all the features it offers.

*2. Maybe you've heard that we cost more than everyone else but . . . .

If your prospect really is concerned with the **_price_**, you might head off their objection by indicating the price hasn't even entered, their mind up to this point. Then the price has now. They may start wondering why you keep mentioning how affordable it is. ***Make a mental inventory of those objections that come.*** Plan to take steps to avoid them. But be careful not to cause an undue anxiety on your prospect's part in the process.

CHAPTER 7

BE PREPARED WITH
TRUSTWORTHY, LOYAL, HELPFUL,
FRIENDLY

"BE PREPARED!" Have you ever dreamed of hiking the wilderness trails that were worn down under moccasin feet hundreds of years ago? Do you hear imagination of the almost noiseless dip-dip of the Indian canoe paddles in the stream where you fish today? Have you stopped to think of the pioneer wagons whose great wheels cut the tracks for our present roads? You can follow those trails, those streams, and tracks. You can have your share of adventure within the *Winners Circle* of salesmanship and the business you seek to win.

It was on a very foggy day in 1909, that *William Boyce,* an American publisher, was searching for an address in old London. All day long the city had been covered with a heavy fog. Street lights had been turned on before noon. Now night was coming on, and it was almost impossible for the stranger to find his way.

Mr. Boyce was surprised when a boy approached and ask if he might be of service. He told the boy where he wanted to go, and was more surprised when the boy saluted him, and said, *"Come with me, Sir."*

Upon reaching the address, Mr. boyce reached into his pocket and offered the a chilling. He was more surprised than ever when the boy refused it. *"No, thank you, sir, I am a Boy Scout. Scouts do not accept tips for Good turns."* The boy told him, and showed him the way to *"Baden-Powell's* office nearby. There, Mr. Boyce found out about the *"Boy Scouts,"* and decided that American boys would like the great game of

Scouting. This was started in America in 1910, a few years before America develop a growing nation. Just like the "*Boy Scouts of America.*"

"*Be Prepared!*" That was and still is the Boy Scout Motto. From the day you become a scout, you set about preparing yourself to help other people. Your ability to help them depends upon how well you learn each Scout skill. Everyday, in countless ways, Scouts, your business, sales and service need to show that they "*Are Prepared*" to point the way.

By putting your *Name Badge* on the right way, is like your business card—you want as many people to remember you as possible. Pin your name badge on your upper right label or shoulder. That way when people reach across to shake your hand, they'll automatically be tuned to get a good view of your name tag. If you don't have a tag, try contacting a uniform facility in your area, and maybe they will have or direct you to someone who does sell them. You may also try sewing your name on those uniforms you received from the same facility for an opportunity from them.

How to improve your sales tools is by following these tips that are especially good for everyone. Try them out when you make the decision to improve the quality of your unique image:

*1.   Redesign your media kit to reflect your unique image.
     This means *adapting* the kit to the area you're working out of.
*2.   Distribute quarterly promotion tools to all customers.
     This means look to *improvise* with the brochures of your sales and service features.
*3.   Update and revise survey studies to help achieve sales goals as the number one product. This means *over come the adjectives,* when you explain how, when and where the program is a better and *up to date* system to control and manage their needs.

If you are looking for ways to maintain high visibility in the local area, follow these guidelines:

*1.   Issue timely press release to a local media. This means, try a "*Penny Saver.*" This may only cost about $20.00 out of your pocket, but with your name, phone number, and a short *ad* regarding your service and product in your area. A lot of referrals will come.
*2.   *Mail Direct-Mail* pieces to target media strengthening awareness of special events, and emphasizing the season.

*3. Review and update media kit material as required. Revise always, as time changes, so does a lot of information.

*4. Develop promotional mailings. This primary for referrals from existing customers.

*5. Coordinate demographic studies. Look up all sales you have sold in the past 2 years as well as services. Identify the areas with the most sales and services. Now plan your promotional mailings to those in the surrounding areas of the existing customers.

*6. Keep in touch with your manager on all competitive media information.

It is always to keep on Track. When you have clear, simple values that everyone understands, it becomes easy to identify gaps between what you believe and how you perform. Thus, real value statements can help yourself "***Walk Their Talk***." When you truly believe in your values, they apply to both your personal and business life. They help you to integrate yourself, rather than be ***schizophrenically split***, where you ferocious in a ***dog-eat-dog*** business environment, but a kind contributor to the community at home.

You have plans. You have a pretty good idea, yourself, of the kind of appointments your should be. But have the manager caught your vision and do they share your ambition? You will find out during the planning sessions of the morning meetings. Here you have a chance to discuss your ideas for the future to get the fellows enthusiastic. You won't go too far in your business, if you always have to turn to someone with a "***What'll we do next?***" The trick is to be full of suggestions for yourself, that you are just bubbling over with them:

*1. "What do you think of a phone call "***Pizza***" meeting to several prospects next Tuesday Night?"

*2. "Would it be a good idea to help with the service and the office staff next month?"

*3. "What about having our next weekly meeting for breakfast at a restaurant or a donut shop?"

Draw out the ideas for what they may have in mind, then settle down with what you have to decide which of the suggestion should be carried out.

In this connection, it is important that you place before your manager and your fellow sales force the programs that you would like have for your business. Of course, your sales force will want to play its part to the full, for the success of all companies undertaking.

In all planning, remember that you would be considered a "*leader*," not the "*boss*," with in your company. You are a *part of the company,* and so is every other sales person. Your business is a small democracy, with everyone having his/her way of being successful, and with the majority vote deciding your actions. President Lincoln's famous words about the government once said, "*of the people, by the people, for the people..*" apply not just the country—they apply to a business, company, and self being.

"*TRUSTWORTHY*"

> Dear Customer:
>
> As a valued member of our service, I take great pride in my work. Part of this pride is shown by ensuring that all services that is delivered to you, is *100 % Customer Satisfaction* in mind.
>
> This service was design by:
> Sales Inspector _____
>
> If you have any questions concerning the contents of this service, please call the number listed below with the sales inspector's name in question.
>
> Customer Service (866) 452-0000
>
> ABC Service Company quarantees customers what they expect, **QUALITY**. Thank You

Our whole world is based on *trusting* other people. You trust the storekeeper from whom you buy your tools to sell you a good one, and the manufacturer who made it to use honest materials. You trust the Post Department when you put a stamp on a letter to deliver it for you. You trust the plumber who mends the kitchen sink to do a good job. Sometimes people fail in their trust, but they live up to it far more often. Unless we trusted people, the whole machinery of living would break down.

As a sales/service inspector, manager, service manager, and even the Region manager know you tell the *truth* and act *honesty* in what you do. If your service in the home broke down, you own up. If you did see someone else failed to correct the service, you tell the truth, even if it means losing the customer.

You do "***exactly a given task***." When your manager ***trust*** you to look after the customer in the absence of the technician, you stay with them. Sometimes an apparently little thing becomes very important. Some years ago, there is always a sales person who wanted to be in the **Winners Circle**. His selling requirements gave him a of trouble. He practiced until he could produce a good sale that passed his company's requirements. Yet, he knew that he had not really mastered his selling. Being trustworthy in what you performed, gives you achievement.

Great Salespeople are Masters of the Art of Persuasion and Trustworthy. **P.T. Barnum,** a trustworthy master salesman and a cofounder of "**Ringling Bros. and Barnum & Bailey**," used to say that "***every crowd has a silver lining.***" Great sales people can see that ***silver lining***—both for themselves and for their customers. They know their product and service, they're ***trustworthy***, and they can still confidence in their customers. Combine these qualities with an ability to listen, to sense through all of the clutter what a customer's hot buttons are; add a passionate determination to put all the ***pieces of the puzzle*** together for the ***features*** and ***benefits*** of the customer, and you've got yourself a great salesperson.

In a lot of ways, the ***Greatest Show On Earth***, is an easy sell.

Everyone loves to be entertained. But we can sell than just shows; i.e. "**We Sell Memories**." We can think of ourselves as being in the "**Wonderment Business,**" and we can take seriously the responsibility of "**Selling Wonderment**," to more than million people a year. At same time, that responsibility makes the selling propositions very exciting.

"LOYALTY"

Loyalty starts in your home and then to your office and business. It shows that you are proud of your family and the teams at your office and business. You appreciate what they do for you. Maybe where you live and your office isn't the finest on the street and the business. Still it is where you live and work, and if you show respect for it, others will too. It is never smart or cleaver to make "***wisecracks***" to others about your home, your family, your team, or your office, as well as your business.

The success of your selling and business depends on the ***loyalty*** of each team member. If you kick, grumble, of fail to pitch in with the team, you are "***disloyal***." If things are not quite to your liking, get to work with the others on the team, and make them ***better***.

A sales, staff, and service teams are loyal to their customers, branch, region, and to the company. Show respect for your ***companies name***, and for its rules and requirements to be successful. You prove your ***loyalty*** by helping in your community and your companies sales and service.

Being a "***Natural Energy Booster***," means, if you're staying up late to be loyal to the company's business, and to finish up any reports, and find your eyelids beginning to droop, avoid caffeine. You'll want to get up out of the chair and get a good night's sleep. Instead, try these refreshers:

*1. Put on snappy, upbeat music.
*2. Take a walk. A brisk ***10-minute*** walk can boost your energy for up to ***two-hours***.
*3. Do some deep breathing.

In most areas of our lives, we function better by **managing Loyalty by agreement** when we have a clear understanding of what's expected in our roles. In business, it's particularly important that we all have a mental understanding of "***rules***." When you have a new member on your team, try to reach a clear understanding at the beginning about expected roles. If possible, write the rules down in a form of a mini-understanding agreement. Before you share them with a new team member, try them out on older team members and get their input on what they think on the agreement should be. If you're daring, do it with your old team members even when you don't have a new member to use it on. It will give to you some interesting insights into how they see your work relationships. As a sales and service team, working with your team gives your company less service cancellations and more sales if you all work with each other. Remember to ***Adapt, Improvise, and Overcome The Objections***.

Loyalty has "***Seven Secrets of Better Persuasion***," when most customers prefer dealing with Sales and Service teams. This is when who are not ***self-centered***, but ***sensitive*** to the feelings of others. Practice these "***Seven Secrets*** to develop ***charisma*** and become a ***powerful persuader***.

*1. Treat everyone you meet as if he or she is the most important person in the world, regardless of how difficult it may seem.
*2. Develop a ***Sensational handshake***. Project a positive thought as you shake hands.
*3. Learn the art of giving ***sincere compliments***. People really do care what you think.

*4. Work on *__your smile__*. When someone smiles back, keep smiling for those magical two extra seconds.

*5. Never *__assume__* people will believe everything you say. Tell them only as much as you think they'll find credible.

*6. The faster you can *__persuade__* people, the more likely you get what you want.

*7. *__Act Consistently__*. People are repelled by people who act contrary to what they say.

Listening to customers is becoming a *__lost art__*. *__So Listen And Earn Loyalty__*. If your business and company is looking for a "*__Fool-Proof__*," way to increase sales, start listening. It happens so rarely these days, when you can actually gain a competitive advantage just by doing it. *__Listening to customers__* is not always easy. If fact, it is the most difficult part of the selling process during the holiday season. When you're selling, your entire focus should be on figuring out what the customer's *__want and then__*, if possible, giving it to them. In the beginning, you don't really know what's best for them at all. There are numerous factors of which you are completely unaware of. It is too easy to *__confuse your needs with theirs__*, particularly when you're trying to make a sale.

In addition to confusion, *__pride and ego__* can also clog up the lines of communication. Always remember to go into a sale or meeting without any *__preconceived notions__* and keep your mind open to anything. Just *__watch, listen, and hear__* what the customer is saying and then make the sale.

Winning sales and service people share many common traits. One of those traits is their willingness and ability to keep detailed records. Losers keep shabby records—or no records at all. What type of records should you keep? Start with "*__written goals and__* "*__monthly sales projections__*." Know if you're on target to reach your monthly goals, or if not, what you need to do. Know what your "*__ratio of contacts__*" to sales is. Keep records of "*__who will buy again__*," when, and how much. Know where your "*__next sale__*," is coming from!

In today's age of low-cost computers and easy-to-learn software programs, there is no excuse for keeping shabby or incomplete records. Records that could help increase your sales.

"HELPFUL"

Within your companies "*__Oath__*," you promised to "*__Help__*" other people at all times. Whether it is just answering a question, follow up on a completion of a sale, and a reinspection on any service performed. The "***Oath***" suggest a definite way to do it—"***the Daily Good Turn***." Start today or this week, to do at least one helpful thing for someone. The logo on the business cards is a symbol of your ***Good Turn***, and you tie a knot with a smile and a handshake to remind you to do it.

At first it may be a little difficult to remember it; you may even have some trouble finding a prospect or an account that will be helpful to someone. But stick to it, and the "***Good Turn***" will soon become a "***Good Habit***." It need not be too large, the spirit is what counts. This ***spirit*** is illustrated by a ***true story by a Pest Control Company*** when something happen one ***Christmas Eve*** several years ago (1983) in the city of Los Angeles, California.

A termite fumigation was schedule on a home where a family of five lived, five days prior to the holidays. Back then, pest control fumigation's took only one day to treat and return back into the house the following day. At the time of the fumigation, there was a small fire that occurred and thus left the family out of the home and the Christmas gifts were all damage. The children were sure, however, that ***Santa Claus*** would still fill their stockings (despite the fire damage) while they all slept at the motel. To the parents, the situation was desperate, because the family needed food and clothing; whereby they were a week or two before they would be able to get back into the home and the insurance company would make arrangements for the repairs. The children chattered of gifts of rollers skates, dolls, and Christmas trees. The parents tried to figured out how to scrape enough together to keep everything going.

Then came a call from the salesperson who sold them the fumigation and had it finance through the company. The salesperson made arrangements for the family to showed up at the company party and that was when the kids shouted "***Santa Claus!***" It was not Santa Claus, but the company staff with their smiles extending clear across there faces. In their arms was an overflow of toys, food and clothing, enough to carry the family through the time needed to get back into their home. the Pest Control Company had heard of the plight of this family and had adopted them as their ***Christmas Good Turn***. As the word got out about them, more prospects started calling in, not to get gifts, but to get ***Help*** with their homes.

There are four (4) ways to ***Help*** you staying motivated:

*1. ***Self-Assessment***: Pinpoint your strength and weakness. Ask yourself what you bring to selling; why you do it.

*2. ***Self-Approval***: This next step is where many of you fall short. It takes a lot of emotional stamina to keep selling day after day, year after year. Read books, listen to inspirational tapes to keep your energy level up and your outlook positive.

*3. ***Self-Commitment***: Once you understand and approve of what you're doing, and why, you need to commit to the actions necessary to produce results.

*4. ***Self-Fulfillment***: When you win a big one, go back to step one—***Self-Assessment***—and ask yourself "What ***Worked***." What areas need ***Improvements***? Remember what work once might not work again. ***Success is cyclic***. You must continually do what needs to be done for ***Self-Fulfillment***.

"FRIENDLY"

The best way to have a "Friend" is to be one. You take a new prospect into your sales goal, and try to make them welcome.

If you are with the service crew, you do your share of the chores and help others if necessary to complete the service. To be a good leader in sales or service, you must first be a ***"Good Friend."*** Make the others in sales or service in the team or the customer know that you care about things that interest them.

A smile helps you to feel ***friendly***. Try it and see. The ***"World-Wide Brotherhood,"*** is based upon ***"friendship."*** To it, belongs sales, service, and office staff that into different branches, have different routes, different selling positions and territories, and may speak different languages. Some go to commercial businesses and rich homes, while others go to families in adequate living and apartment housing. But within your company, you are all friends and brothers, though you from all corners of the earth.

Creating friendly coaching relationships has six (6) aspects:

*1. Create a coaching contract that essentially says that you have permission to help coach the new sales or service person's on your teams.

*2. Find out what the new sales or service person's sincere and honest intention is and align your intention with it.

*3. Give the new sales or service person the gift of your presence by setting a time and place to hold a coaching conversation. i.e. Maybe a donut shop in the morning or hamburger place for lunch.

*4. The primary medium for all coaching intervention is conversation at a morning meeting.

*5. To have an empowering coaching team relationship, you should recognize that sales or service person have the inherent creativity, intelligence, and tacit knowledge that need to succeed but may need help in gaining access to it.

*6. Be willing to discuss the undiscussable.

Stating the problem as a "*friendly*" question can have many definitions, while a problem definition works well if it ends with a friendly question mark. A friendly question invites an answer from the customer. "*to develop a plan to obtain new service treatment*" is not as effective as "*What do we have to do to get this new service treatment started?*" "*How can we sell more ABC service?*" yields more ideas than "*Developing a marketing plan to increase ABC services.*" If you need to *prime to pump*, use any of the following to get the creative juices flowing:

*1. "*How*" suggest a process.
*2. "*Where*" directs us to locations.
*3. "*Who*" identifies the people involved.
*4. "*When*" points to time when is needed.
*5. "*What*" sorts out process and service needed.

A *Friendly Image Making—Appearance is everything.* An image comes slowly over time. There are many ways you and your team can develop your own *special image*. These include:

*1. *Printed materials*—As a team member, your company can't afford to ignore even the smallest detail in the category. One of the most important printed pieces is your *business cards*. A business card says a great deal about a business, and it is often the first and only thing potential customers see. These days, you can do a lot of *creative things* with business cards, if you have help from a good artist and printer. They will also incorporate your special message and logo onto stationary, letterhead, pamphlets and brochures. In general, if you want to convey the image of a "*no-nonsense*" operation, keep our printed materials subdued and business like. This doesn't mean boring, however. Use quality paper stock, make your logo prominent, and use boldface type when starting a proposal letter.

*2. **_The Spoken Word_**—Many times, taking your message directly to the public is better than putting it into print. Everytime you speak at a meeting, a proposal presentation at a company breakfast meeting, or network at a family get together, you are personalizing your business by presenting your position to face to face. Don't ever underestimate the **_power of word of mouth_** as a tool for **_advertising, promoting,_** and **_enhancing_** your business. You can call yourself a **_"true humanitarian,"_** but unless you get out there and help the homeless or another charitable cause, no one will believe you. You may want to be known as "**_The Expert within your Industry_**," but no one will know until you present yourself at meetings. In other words, your business should be **_an extension of yourself_**.

*3. **_Visual Elements_**—A **_friendly image_** is most of all **_visual_**. Films, graphic displays, videos, recommendations, are all part of making a **_visual image_**. Videos are used in all facets of business. Videos demonstrates the procedures of preparing the customer the advantage of your business programs. Graphic displays are used to explain the facets of the preparation needed to complete your business programs. Graphic displays also explain the facets of the procedures on where and what needs to complete the program.

Building an friendly image takes **_time_** and **_careful_** planning.

If you know who your prospect is, and what they want from you, you are ahead of the game. For instance, you are preparing your customer for your company service. Take the customer through the structure and demonstrate along with the copy of the graph of the structure.

The next step—**_defining_** what your image should be—involves taking a good look at your business and/or service, and deciding how it would best fit in the safe keeping of the structure.

The final step—**_establishing_** your image—is an ongoing process. Remember that any time you distribute printed materials, appear and speak in public, or produce any visual aids, you are helping to project and maintain the **_friendly image you desire_**!

CHAPTER 8

BE PREPARED WITH
COURTEOUS, KIND, OBEDIENT &
CHEERFUL

"COURTEOUS"

Courteous is just another way of saying "_A Salesperson is a lady and/ or a gentlemen_. Courtesy comes from the heart, and goes _hand in hand_, with _friendship_.

The caveman was all right in his day. He squatted beside his fire, snatched his lump of meat, pulled it apart with his hands and teeth. If he saw anything he wanted, he grabbed it. If someone was in his way, he knocked him down.

But who wants a caveman around today? Especially in your house, company and office. Along with houses, tables, knives and forks and in the company's office, coffee, references, and teamanship, we have develop standards of friendship and courtesy which make life a lot more enjoyable.

Part of the training of pleads at **West Point** and **Annapolis**, includes training in the courtesies of "_an officer and a gentleman_." The company you build, the training of the *"Winner's Circle,"* includes training in the courtesies of "_a team member in outstanding leadership and performance_.

Among your company's team, there are four "_Courteous Tips On Teaming_:

*1. Select a facilitator/moderator to monitor progress and maintain momentum.

*2. Invest in the necessary tools so that team members can participate fully.

*3. Set up training sessions for team members. Group sessions will boost both learning and team-building.

*4. Make time to build relationships among team members. Look for opportunities at morning meetings.

Here are two questions and answers on building a business, base upon **_Courteously_**

*1. **_Question_**—How long will it be before we see some results? **_Answer_**—It really depends on the sales you are making to get to the **_Winner's Circle_** within your company. It usually takes 3-5 years before sales people learn how to really work together as a team. If lots of training and support are provided, you could see improvements as soon as **_18 months_**. Most sales people at your business should go through stages:
   * Recognizing that teams are possible;
   * Learning how teams function;
   * Learning the necessary skills;
   * Internalizing what they've learned so teams are formed automatically whenever the **_Winner's Circle_** require them.

*2. **_Question_**—How should team members be disciplined? **_Answer_**—Teams have, especially **_Winner's Circle Sales People_**, a crack at fixing their own problems. If someone isn't listening to the team, or respecting its decisions, it's best to have a team member meet with that person and let him/her know his/her behavior is causing problems. A courteous call always helps and maybe improve the team effort.

It is always difficult to decide how you want to be paid as a sales representative. This is how **_Courteously Speaking Representative Talk_** comes into play. There are several steps to consider, however, that make this easier. **_First_**, you need to determine if you want to be in the **_Winner's Circle_**, or just another representative. There are pluses and minuses to each. Then, remember to always calculate commissions on your gross profit and remember the requirements to meet the **_Winner's Circle._** The ideal time to pay commissions is when the customer pays; so maybe stop by and pick it up and ask for a referral. It's probably worth considering using sales quotas. Finally, be sure to document all your compensation plans carefully to avoid disagreements later on.

All Sales Team's have a "***Bill Of Rights***" to ***Courteously***.

*1. You have the right to refuse a request from a customer without feeling guilty, knowingly that it may cause damage to their property.

*2. You have the right to feel reasonably express anger, especially when you did not make the monthly sales quota.

*3. You have the right to feel and express healthy competitiveness, especially when you did make the monthly sales quota.

*4. You have the right to use your judgment on which needs are more important to you when a conflict arises between your work and your professional life.

*5. You have the right to have feelings respected and considered by prospects, customers, and business alike. Remember, being positive of what you produce, will be rewarded with feelings.

*6. You have the right to make mistakes without feeling guilty. Admitting to all, will show your confidence.

*7. You have the right to be treated as a capable human adult, and to not be patronized.

*8. You have the right to ***courtesy*** and respect that you earned as a human being.
AND LAST BUT NOT LEAST—

*9. You have the right not to be ***perfect*** but still try get the "***Winner's Circle Recognition***."

Here are "***Six Commandments of Courtesy***," to take you from be just ***O.K.,*** to being one of the "***Elite Super Stars in The Winner's Circle :***

*1. ***See the big picture.*** Selling isn't only about ***trading cash*** for ***service***. It's about listening, meeting needs, and developing relationships.

*2. ***Do the right thing.*** Let you conscience guide you. If you believe in winning at the cost, you're doomed to lose.

*3. ***Don't make excuses.*** Take total responsibility for your actions. It's amazing how simple life becomes when you do it.

*4. ***Stay hungry.*** You can't be great if you're happy with being good. Strive to keep learning, and always try new things.
*5. ***Just do it.*** Great ideas don't mean a thing if you don't execute them.
*6. ***Work, Work, work, work!*** If you want to **<u>win</u>** you have work **<u>harder and smarter</u>** than everyone else.

"KIND"

Naturally you are **<u>Kind</u>** to pets, the family cat, the dog, to the poultry, and the farm livestock; not to forget the business technicians, the office staff, the boss, and customers' family home, business and the animals around their property. As a **<u>Winner's Circle Super Star</u>**, your care should extend further. As you study your business, then wild animals, birds, and insects, you will become as much interested in protecting and helping them as you are in the animals around the customer's home and business when you are in the pest control business. You can set up a service that is safe to the customers with recommendations that will help them with a smile and a thank you in their needs. Perhaps with others on your team, you can take part in a state pest control conversation project. Nevertheless, starting out being ***kind*** with the customer's needs in what ever their desire is, can bring you to the ***Winner's Circle.***

Are you steeling your nerves to ask "Kindly" for a raise?

If you didn't start planning for this moment a year ago, you may not be successful. In these tough economic times, a raise isn't granted automatically just because a year has passed. You have to prove your worth to the company. Show that you've **<u>made</u>** or **<u>saved company's</u>** money and you're a likely candidate for a raise.

At your next performance review (a new years resolution), set the stage for next years' raise. The **<u>document your efforts</u>**. This means you have to **<u>measure and track your progress and results</u>**. You can do the following:

*1. Bring in new customers.
*2. Win over angry customers.
*3. Build in quality to a procedure.
*4. Volunteer to help during an emergency.
*5. Look for a new way to reach customers.
*6. Make sure your projects are completed on time.

Increase your probability for success by **_Kindness_** by preparing yourself for **_goal setting_** is **_important_**.

*1. **_Create A Positive Kind Image_**—Learn to paint a positive picture of yourself. Don't harp on your mistakes. See them as learning opportunities that will help you do better in the future.

*2. **_Build Control and Confidence_**—Look for a job that provides you with opportunities to control at least part of your environment and in which you will receive some recognition.

*3. **_Don't be a perfectionist_**—Think realistically. Don't set impossible standards for yourself. No one in this world is perfect. Acknowledge your strengths and weaknesses.

*4. **_Accept help kindly_**—Be ready to accept help kindly when you need it. Everyone has areas in which you can improve. Seek help kindly from those **_team members_** who have **_knowledge and abilities_** that will complement yours. Don't feel **_guilty or weak_**. Most people will be flattered by the request.

*5. **_Accept your own achievements kindly_**—Don't fall prey to the *"impostor syndrome"* (where you feel you don't deserve your success). Evaluate your performance against your goals and you'll see you've earned whatever gains you've made.

*6. **_Learn to say no kindly_**—You can be nice without allowing others to dump their work or their problems on you. You should decide **_who, where, when, and how_** much to give. Remember to be **_kind_** to others.

Kindly think of *"**Positive Mindset**"* in changes. In the pursuit of continuous improvement, every individual, from a technician to salesperson, must surrender the beliefs that have long been nurtured in some companies. You must embrace new beliefs in the coming year that cal for dramatically different **_concepts_** and **_behavior_**.

SURRENDER	*EMBRACE*
* The feeling of having learned it all.	* Learning never stops.
* Thinking about task in isolation.	* Thinking about systems.
* Relying on procedures.	* Focus on Results.
* Searching for simplicity.	* Existence of complexity
* Placing blame on "**_them_**."	* Personal responsibility.

* Virtue of being certain.   * Existence of doubt.
* Belief in stability.   * Continuous change.

Customers judge you kindly when you following the top seven examples of ***good customers service***, as seen by the customer, as seen by the customer.

*1.   Genuine company greetings, like "***How are you doing today***?" or "***Welcome to ABC Company***."
*2.   ***Smiling Salesperson***. You only have eight seconds to make a good first impression.
*3.   ***Available Salesperson***. If you're not with another customer, drop what you're doing to greet and assist a lead.
*4.   ***Knowledgeable Salesperson***. ***Study, Study, Study***. You need to be able to readily show all ***features and benefits*** of your service and company proposal.
*5.   ***A clean appearance***. Good housekeeping of your appearance and your company's vehicle will enhance your company's image.
*6.   ***Useful suggestions***. Help customers confirm their needs and choices.
*7.   ***A visible manager***. Your company's sales and service managers are their to give you and your customers some assistance with authority to answer questions.

The "***Art Of Persuasion,***" is someone to take a particular action, trying ***kindly*** to do the following:

*1.   Know what you want.
*2.   Know exactly what your request entails.
*3.   Be able to list several benefits to the other person if they take the action you want.
*4.   Anticipate possible objections. Then decide how and when to present the information.

Remember that the best situation is to ***Win-Win***, where they benefit as much as you do from taking the action you need.

Communication is when you deal with other people. It is helpful to know their "***Style***." Here's a new way of organizing communication styles:

*1. The **_Noble Category_** is direct and straight forward, including people who say what they think and try to avoid emotion.

*2. The **_Socratic Style_** is verbose and detail-oriented. They talk out their entire thought process.

*3. The **_Reflective Style_** listens a lot and tries to keep things warm and supportive.

While we can vary our **_Styles_**, we tend toward certain patterns.

Say "**_You're Good_**, Say **_You're Kind_**, and **_You'll Be Better_** when rating yourself on your work. Take the benefit of the doubt and rate yourself higher. People who rate themselves high have more **_self-esteem_**, are happier with their sales and or service position, and have fewer physical complaints than people who rate themselves lower than their bosses do. So, stand up and say—"**_I'm Good ! I'm Kind ! I'm Better_** !!!

"OBEDIENT"

After George Washington had successfully defeated the British Army, an officer asked his mother how she manage to raise so brilliant son? You know Washington's character, his fame for truth, his honor, his bravery. But his mother's reply to the question touched none of these qualities. She answered "**_I taught him to obey!_**"

This was not only the case with Washington. The great men of history learned to obey when they were young. They learned to **_discipline_** themselves before they could give orders to others. **_Obedience is a persons quality_**. It shows **_self-control, strength of character_**. Great men and women know how to take orders. Weaklings whine and grumble about them.

Obedience is something everyone has to learn. How successful would your company's winner's circle team be if the rest of the sales and service team disobeyed their coach's (manager's) instructions, and ignored their positive signals? What fun would you have on a "**_Pizza Night Customer Calling Party_** if half the team straggled off the road, and the rest had to waste the afternoon looking them up?

If everyone is to have a good time in the Winner's Circle Team, or in life, and successfully in winning for the year; you need to learn first to take orders and carry them out, **_cheerfully and promptly_**. Remember to **_Adapt, Improvise, and Overcome The Objectives_**.

Promoting _**Obedience**_ in the "_**Positive Attributes**_" of growing older, you'll want to consistently sell to the "_**50+**_" crowd. You must first recognize the positive aspects associated with aging namely:

*1. _**More control over one's time**_. Older buyers, especially those who are retired, live more control over their time than at any other period in their lives. This opens the door to some special sales opportunities.

*2. _**Wisdom, experience, and maturity**_. G. Stanley Hall once said, "_**There is a certain maturity of judgment about and women, things, causes, and life generally that nothing in the world but years can bring—real wisdom that only age can teach.**_" Recognize this, believe it, and act accordingly.

*3. _**Achievement, Accomplishment**_. It takes many years of hard work to achieve anything of substance in life. The overwhelming majority of millionaires in America (75%) are over 50 years old.

*4. _**The Opportunity To Give To Others**_. This is a time when people can give of themselves to society. The over 50's are actively involved in a wide spectrum of political, social, and spiritual causes.

Believe it or not, _**Obedience**_ give some good things that come from conflict. If you can avoid the negative emotional entanglements by the following conflicts:

*1. _**Conflict**_ gives you a clear signal that people are unhappy, thus it's a last ditch form of communication.

*2. _**Conflict**_ forces you to look at ways to improve prove the system. It can encourage you to make changes.

*3. _**Conflict**_ gives you a chance to resolve it well, thus making everybody feel closer than ever.

*4. _**Conflict**_ with yourself encourages you to change your own behaviors (for instance, if you know smoking is bad for you, and it creates a mental conflict).

Going to a "_**Convention,**_" where you want to be _**obedient**_ and develop sales leads, are important to improve your productivity:

*1. _**Plan and Prepare Obedience**_—Develop a plan before you go. Have realistic goals for the number of contacts you'll make and how you'll make them. Even go a day early. This will leave you relaxed and energized when the convention starts. You can also make contact with people setting up their exhibits. Maybe give them some of your cards.

*2. **_Seek Out Others_**—Look for others and see what their common goal is as well.

*3. **_Make Contact with The New And The Old_**—Have a list of important contacts you want to meet. Make a point to go to their talks or to see them in other settings.

*4. **_Socialize_**—There are good settings for getting to know your target contacts informally.

"CHEERFUL"

Do you know that a fellow who is all smiles as long as he or she gets what they wants, but who grouses like a spoiled child, if they don't. A person likes to sell a good job on a fine day, but not when the wind blows the dust in their eyes. A person is a good pal as long as you help them in selling what they want. A person is smiling in the "**_Winner's Circle_**" if his manager offers the team a "**_Hot Tip for the Day;_**" but if the manager wants the collections collected, the team doesn't act like one.

You have live long enough to know that you can't have your way all the time. You also realize that you are going to have to do a certain number of things you don't particularly like. **_Everyone has to. All right, face it, be cheerful about it._** You'll make your home duties, company office work or any other job easier and pleasanter if you are pleasant. The time will pass more quickly and the job be easier. **_Cheerfulness_** is more or less a habit. It will help you a lot to have more friends, and enjoy life and your company's business.

In producing a quality service, **_perfectionism_** has considerable value. We all remember stories of **_Mrs. Fields_** throwing out an entire batch of cookies because something about them wasn't right.

It's this kind of **_cheerful perfectionism_** which tells all in your team that you really mean it when you say you want **_high quality_**. Your **_#1_** customer is an internal one in your company. If you allow shoddy work to get by, it will be reflected in how your services team treat your external customers.

If others lie about you or blame you for problems to give themselves an edge, take the backstabbers by surprise "**_Cheerfully._**" Use public confrontation, but be **_calm, direct, and pick a time_** when the other person isn't prepared. Simply state the facts and ask them to stop because their behavior is bad for the company.

When **_Obsession Works Cheerfully_**, team members who are obsessed, get more done. You educate yourself, you work hard, and you show **_enthusiasm_**. This inspires others. Usually obsession starts when you **_love something_**—like a hobby or sport. Apply this passion to your work. Become obsessed with learning a new skill or learning all there is to know about how customers feel. **_Ask Questions_**. Pay attention to every detail. We begin to like what we learn more about. Take a new area and become more interested in it. Cultivate your ability to become obsessed with aspects of your work, and you'll become a more passionate "**_Winner's Circle Team Member_**." **_Improve Your Listening Skills Cheerfully By The Following Rules_**:

*1.   An old rule but a good one: **_Listen more than you speak_**.
*2.   Try to clear your mind of your own worries and thoughts so you can truly listen to what is being said.
*3.   **_Don't interrupt or finish the other prospect's sentences._**
*4.   **_Avoid Assumptions_**. Don't jump to conclusions about what the other prospect is saying.
*5.   **_Show Interest_**. Make eye contact with the speaker, use facial expressions, and rephrase what has been said.
*6.   **_Be Honest_**. If you are short on time, let the prospect know and make arrangements to meet later.

Office **_Politics_** can be performed **_Cheerfully_**. Learning the industry is important and sometimes requires some "**_Political Know How_**." Here are some great tips about office politics and what you can do to get ahead:

*1.   Seek out several mentors, and perhaps with different areas of expertise. Not everyone will open to mentoring you. Many will be susceptible to flattery, time, and attention from you.
*2.   **_Form An Extensive Network_**. Make friends and political allies all over the company. It can take months, or even years, to build a relationships, but that's what business and life are all about.
*3.   **_Get Honest feedback_**. It's sometimes hard to get clear feedback from your service or sales manager. Try team members and others who work with you. Even if the feedback is wrong, it's right. It is important to be sensitive to how other team members perceive you.

*4. **_Reach Out To Everyone_**. Don't build bridges to the team above you. Team members can also be important. Team members under you (such as an technicians or secretary) can be great sources of information and can help you get lots of proposals done through referrals on the projects they just did for you.

*5. **_Don't Be Afraid To Toot Your Own Horn_**. Let team members you accomplish something. Don't **_Brag_**, but make the team aware of your efforts of the company. If you can get other team members to plug you, even better.

There are **_"Five Characteristics Of A Cheerfully Good Deadline."_** Most of us live and work be deadlines. What makes an effective and useful deadline? Here are **_Cheerful Five Hints_**.

*1. **_It's Realistic_**—The act of making a deadline should force you to realistically assess the time and effort required to meet it.

*2. **_It's Specific_**—Never use deadlines that call for you to **_make some real progress_**. On a new prospect, or "**_make people aware_**" of the unfamiliar procedure. These vague aims are frustrating, because they don't imply specific results. When you set a deadline, be sure it's concrete and measurable.

*3. **_It's Understandable_**—Don't set a deadline until and unless you're familiar with the steps required to meet it.

*4. **_It's sequential_**—Good deadlines are usually the composite of a series of sequential action steps. As you complete or master each step, you can put it aside and go on to the next.

*5. **_It's Challenging_**—Good deadlines involve a bit of challenge. They should motivate you to undertake a task with a bit more efficiency and creativity than you've used in the past.

Selling and appointment **_Cheerfully_** is where nobody wants to waste their time having a salesperson "**_Sell Them_**." Everyone has some needs in the marketplace. A salesperson always wants to have a **_direct and honest_** approach to get an appointment. Say something like "**_I can only be successful if I help customers. If you'll invest the time exchange information at lunch, I'll try to give you some information of value. If I can't help you, I'll tell you that too. Is that fair enough_**?"

If you cannot help handle the **_disagreements_** when they first come out. The key is to be **_Cheerfully Pleasant_**. You can:

*1. ___*Clarify The Disagreements*___. Most are based upon simple misunderstandings. Make sure you actually disagree.

*2. ___*Be Polite*___. Sarcasm escalates the conflict..

*3. Don't embarrass prospects or fellow team members in the public.

*4. ___*Don't Just Criticize someone You Disagree With*___. Propose alternatives. Try to come up with one you can both get together on.

CHAPTER 9

BE PREPARED WITH
THRIFTY, BRAVE, CLEAN & REVERENT

"THRIFTY"

Every person wants to pay their own way in everything they do. You work to earn the money to help buy your supplies and equipment for household family needs, as well as business. Take good care of the things that belong to you, your vehicle, and other items that represent money. Make them last as long as possible. On training seminars, commercial prospects, and on business trips; be careful not to waste money to impress others. Take only what you need and present what they will want. Real thrift on all business prospects is not just saving money. It is saving with a purpose and spending wisely the money your prospect wants to save.

Thrift actually consist of *Four Thrifty Items*:

*1. *Earning*
*2. *Saving*
*3. *Spending Wisely*
*4. *Sharing*

It takes hard work to earn money as a *Winner's Circle Team Leader*. When you work for it, you appreciate it. If you save it toward your *future ambition*, you are saving with a purpose. When you spend it, spend it *carefully and wisely*. Remember always try to share what you have with those less fortunate than you. A team leader has plenty to show what they have achieved to others on their *teams*

There are ***Four Steps*** to ***Sustaining*** a learning process and establishing ***Thriftiness***.

*1. Established a compelling link between the current behavior of the team and the company's results for which it is responsible.

*2. Help fellow team members to see that despite good intentions, your team may often produce unintended consequences due to lack of awareness.

*3. Help fellow team members to see that it is possible to learn to think and act in ways that reduce defensive routines and increase effectiveness in dealing with company's business issues.

*4. Create a frame for intervening through the governing values and ground rules. The following list recaps the governing values:

*   A free and informed choice in regard to setting goals, methods, and changing one's behavior.

*   Authentic communication and sharing of valid information.

*   Internal commitment to outcomes, and

*   Learning is a sacred as results. Ground rules include things like "***focus on interest, not positions***," "***no cheap shots***," and "***separate team members from the problems***."

Being "***Thrifty***," can sometimes encourage creativity by stimulating a very simple thing. For example, "***Wagner***" composed his best music while stroking velvet, ***Emile Zola*** worked best in artificial light and would pull his shades down during the day to work, ***Picasso*** could not paint well unless someone else was in the room with him. Experiment with everything for possible big increases in ***on the job*** creativity. Demonstrate service to the person in charge, knowingly that their business is filled with clients seeking other needs.

Once you received the business, follow a "***Thrifty Way***" on referrals.

*1. ***Thank the customer who referred you***, by sending a hand written note within 24 hours, thanking the customer who made the referral.

*2. ***Contact the referral within 24 hours.*** The ***24 hour*** limit has to do with you and your thinking. The longer you wait to make the contact, the less important the referral seem.

*3. ***Report back to the customer who referred you.*** No matter which way it goes—sale or no sale-appointment or not—report back within **_72 hours_**. This shows that the referral was important to you, and it also demonstrates your follow-through capabilities.

"***Time Management***," is a thrifty way to take care of things that belong to you. It makes you last as long on prospects as possible. Here are some great tips that will give you a long range of benefits:

*1. Review your long-range goals **_DAILY_**.
*2. Make sure that your current activity is in line with what you really want to accomplish.
*3. Prioritize what you need to do, both in terms of actual importance, and time urgency.
*4. Record and analyze how you spend your time.
*5. Make sure your first hour at work gets something done to give you momentum for the day.
*6. Look for continual improvement in how you do things to work smarter, not harder.
*7. Schedule quiet time every day.
*8. Learn to say, "**_NO_**."
*9. Make your "**_To Do_**" list for tomorrow today.

"BRAVE"

In 1947, a fourteen-year Boy Scout performed such an outstanding act of **_bravery_** that newspapers all across the country printed the story. He was a ***"Star Scout"*** of Syracuse, New York, and he saved the life of a child from a burning launch. To do this, he had to swim twice under a patch of blazing oil. From his boat, he dived in an swam under the flames. He climbed aboard the blazing launch, and holding the child with one arm and keeping his other hand over her nose and mouth to prevent her from inhaling the water. He dive again and swam with her **_twenty-five feet_** under the water covered with blazing oil, to safety. For this extraordinary act of courage, the ***National Court of Honor of the Boy Scouts of America*** awarded him a **_Gold Medal with Crossed Palms_**.

Thousands of other Scouts have shown extraordinary bravery and quick thinking in times of danger. Their Scout skills have given them the knowledge which help them saved a life. Their character as Scouts has helped give them courage to do so.

Perhaps as a company *"Team Member,"* you will not have the opportunity to prove your bravery in such a fashion. But there are test of your bravery that you face every day when you proposed a restrictive or risky service on a residence, apartment complex, condominiums, commercial complexes and housing or businesses built so close to each other.

You know the ideals of the laws or promises made. You know right from wrong, and in spite of urging and *"wise cracks,"* you can do what is right. You can be brave in the face of danger, and brave in the face of temptation.

Remember, those who believe they can move mountains, do. Those who believe they can't-cannot. Belief triggers the power to do. And the power is always the success in achieving your goals.

"CLEAN"

You know how good you feel after a bath, with plenty of soap and hot water. As a company's Team member, you keep clean in thought and speech too, and the feeling is just as satisfying. Keeping clean in body is part of being ***physically strong***. Keeping clean in thought, speech and habits is necessary to be ***morally straight***.

A little soap and water and rubbing will remove the dirt from the outside of your body. But no soap, will remove dirt that gets inside in your ***mind***.

The best way to keep clean in ***thought, word*** and ***actions***, is to go with those team members who are trying to do the same thing. Being in the ***Winner's Circle Team Member***, who are trying to do the same thing. Be ***mentally***, if your team members are the right sort.

You will find if you do your best to live up to the company's rules and regulations, and if you live an active, worthwhile life. It will be easier to keep clean in ***thought and action***.

Team members who hang around some of the offices or waste their time in other ways are the ones generally who have time for dirty stories, thoughts and lack of ambition to be a team member in the *"**Winner's Circle**. The team members who keeps busy with worthwhile ambition, who is thrifty with their time and their energies, is also ***clean in their thoughts and actions***. So, it is always best to be a ***Team Member In The Winner's Circle***.

The keys to successful proposal packaging are getting the prospect's attention and giving them a reason to read the rest of the proposal. If you avoid typical openers and get straight to how to the prospect benefits, your proposals will stand apart from the others, dramatically increasing chances of communicating your ***sales messages***.

The best opening sentences do more than grab attention. They draw the prospect into the proposal. When you're making a statement, be sure it ties in with ***what you're selling***. If you ask a question, be sure the answer plays in your favor. For example:

*1. "Can you think of a better way to keep track of our service schedules, so that we can see all your tenants and treat a building?" Is this risky? The prospect may be able to think of many better ways. A safer bet:

*2. "Would direct scheduling and tenant meetings on a weekly basis, give us a better way of controlling our service schedule on each building complex?"

Chances are high the answer will be "***Yes***."

Effective ***paraphrasing*** brings needs and wants out into the open and solicits agreements from prospects and co-workers. Practice paraphrasing statements that other prospects make with words that ***real unexpected meanings*** and ***feelings***. After paraphrasing, always check their reactions by adding a ***tie-down*** at the end. Here are some more practical examples of the technique:

Answering a Customer's response:
*   "I just never get around to doing what needs to be done."

Your Paraphrase:
*   "In other words, you need something to help you get organized and save you time with our service. Is that right?"

Chances are high the answer will be "***Yes***."

Your Customer's Feelings:
*   "Business is slow. And I know that I'll have to cut back on spending."

Your Paraphrase back:

*   It sounds as if you need to improve your ability to make more money, but canceling our service will decrease your ability to increase your profits. And that's what you really want, isn't it?"

Chances are high the answer will be "***No***."

When opening verbal clean shots, a straight sale's approach using a prospect-oriented statement is . . . .

*   "Most likely to succeed," there was only one thing left for me to do; tell you how our company's business can help turn "***likely***" into certain.

To get an appointment when the prospect won't return your phone call; use a questions . . . .

*   "You obviously recognize the benefits of this company for your commercial management complex's. won't you take a closer look at ours and imagine what your business tenants will do for your safety in your complex's.

Apology approach using empathy and "***Humility***" with the prospect-oriented statement and question . . . .

*   "Mr. Jones, your disappointment at how our proposal has been handled is understandable, especially in light of your commercial management reputation for excellence. Since there's no good excuse for our poor performance, may I make up to you with this ***offer***?"

Straight sales approach using customer-oriented benefit statement.

*   "Mr. Smith, reliable service in your management is more than just a phrase; it's the difference between success and failure.

That's why you need our company service that really delivers."
Cover approach with an article about competitor's use of the service.

* "It is possible to have our company's constant access to your complex's and keep cost down. Our competitors can prove it every day."

Selling against your competition in a cleanly manner, can be done by the following:

*1. Know what claims your competitors are making about their service.
*2. Know what negative claims your competitors are making about your service. Answer those objections up front in your presentation.
*3. Know your competitors; vulnerable points. Stress points about your service that you know they can't match.
*4. Avoid attacking your competitors' service or products.
*5. Never make personal attacks.
*6. Never criticize your prospect for considering doing business with a competitor.
*7. Show how your service and product is better. Not how your competitor's is worse.
*8. Emphasize those features and benefits of your product/ service that your competitor(s) can't match.

When marketing your "Customer Appreciation Cleanliness," ask yourself, are you overlooking the best source of business—your existing customer? Marketing to current customers cost less than targeting new ones and plays off better, too. Just asked around and talk to any "**Winner's Circle Team Member**" in any pond, on how this can reveal that it is keeping clients coming back for more. They will say:

*1. Position yourself as an invaluable resource. alert customers to seminars, trade shows, or magazines they might find relevant. Whenever you think of a way to save clients money or enhance their productivity, let them know more about your service or products.
*2. Give something for _free_. Offer a free service or a discount coupon as a reward for continued business.
*3. Provide clients with referrals. People always appreciate new leads, and giving referrals conveys your value to customers in a tangible way. For instance, provide a real estate agent a lead that one of

your customers is about to sell their business or home and are looking for an agent vs. the agent giving you an escrow service.

*4. Make your clients stars. With the permission, why not hang your customers' photos in your place of business.

*5. Maintain visibility through writing. If you don't already send a company newsletter to clients, consider doing so.
Or offer to write articles in industry publications your clients.

*6. Another way to retain your clients, provided you have a home or business computer. Try using the ___Internet Web Site Card program___. This is one of the best ___advertisement___ features to those who are out there and constantly looking for marketing their own service via the ___Internet E-Mail PowerPoint service file___.

Just like Moses, who handed down the ___10 Commandments___ to all at the base of Mt. Sini; there are 10 **Good and Clean Commandments of Customer Relations.** They are:

*1. Customers are deserving of the most attentive and courteous treatment we can give.

*2. Customers are the people who makes it possible for us to pay our salaries, whether we are office employees, Team Members, or managers.

*3. A customer is not someone to argue or match wits with.

*4. Customers do not depend on us; rather, we are dependent upon them.

*5. Customers are part of our business—not outsiders. They are not interruptions of our work, they are the purpose of it.

*6. Customers are not cold statistics—they are flesh and blood human being with feelings and emotions like our own.

*7. Customers are the lifeblood of this and every other business.

*8. A customer is the important person in any business.

*9. Customers do us a favor when they call—we are not doing them a favor by serving them.

*10. A customer likes to trade with the ___Winner's Circle Team Member___ who supports the community.

Follow these commandments every day and you will become a follower who made it to be the "___Kingdom Of The Winner's Circle Team Members___." You too may have followers seeking wisdom from you in the future.

"*REVERENT*"

A **_Super Star In The Winner's Circle_** who is truly "**_Reverent_**" toward the holly spirit who shows reverence in every day actions as well as the activities in the sacred holly place. Your own spiritual guide's leader will tell you how to practice reverence according to the teachings of your religion.

Some team members think they are smart by referring to people of other religions or other races by **_unkind nicknames_**.

They think it not realize that their own religion and customs may seem strange to someone else also. For the rest of your selling life, you should be associating with customers and prospects of different religious beliefs and customs. It is **_your duty_** to respect customers and prospects for their beliefs, and train yourself to respect others for what they are and what they do, instead of being influenced by their color or creed.

Color and religious beliefs are no basis for judging a customer or a prospect. All **_Customers and Prospects_** were created by same Holly Spirit, and all are equal before the **_provider of life_**. By living up to the company rules, by doing good to your fellow team members, customers and future prospects, you are doing your duty as a **_Winner's Circle Team Member_**.

There are **_Three Deadly Advertising Mistakes_** to the referrals. They are:

*1. Failure to be **_simple_** and **_clear_**.
*2. Failure to be **_direct_**.
*3. Failure to follow the fundamentals.

Unless you as team members are **_simple, clear, and direct_**, you don't communicate. You are not understood. And if you stray from the **_fundamentals_**, your chances for success are remote, at best. You need to ask, "**_What is the deal_**?" and "**_What is in it for me_**?" You answer those questions fast. **_Very Fast_**. We need to be direct to **_communicate_** immediately and unmistakably that we do have news of interest and benefits to the customers and prospects. **_This is good advertising_**!!!

Power Performance has "**_Secrets_**." Power Performers need to know the following:

*1. Make their lives an adventure.
*2. Take charge of their lives.
*3. Always know they have choices.

*4. Experience success long before they achieve it.
*5. Don't let other people drag them down to their level.
*6. Know that for things to change, they have to change.
*7. Know how to make money work for them.
*8. Learned how to enhance their time.
*9. Know how to create opportunities.
*10. Learned how to turn their fear into fortune.
*11. Learned how to put love, respect into their lives.

As generally speaking, here are ***20 Religious Ways To Make Your Closing Much More Successful To Reach Your Goals***:

*1. Don't rush the sales cycle.
*2. Don't underestimate the importance of prospecting.
*3. Monitor your prospecting results. Do 20 completed calls result in at least ***five*** scheduled appointments. Do those ***five*** schedule appointments result in a least one sale.
*4. If you're finding that, over and over again, you're losing sales because of the same ***objection***;—say, that your price is ***too high***,—you are probably facing some problem on an organizational level. Take the time to talk to your sales manager about company's strategies and market position.
*5. Once you have made contact by telephone, build your ***first-in-person*** visit upon your past discussion with the contact. Don't begin from scratch as though you'd never spoken with your contact before! If possible and appropriate, mention some memorable element or remark from the earlier phone conversation. This will move the ***prospect*** away from the "***it's-time-to-talk-to-some-team member***" mindset and toward the "***this-is-that-interesting-person-from-that-interesting-company***" mindset.
*6. Don't obsess (to occupy the mind) on an single account. If a team member devotes to visit a prospect account more than a dozen times before closing, this may sound impressive. But what if the time that you spent on the call could have been devoted to prospecting efforts that would have led you to three or quite possibly more sales.
*7. ***Don't try to present during the interview state.***
*8. Don't confuse a presentation with a demonstration. The presentation is what you do after you've gotten all the information

you need from the prospect during your interviewing stage. A demonstration of company's service may take place much earlier. It's something you do to elicit interest at an earlier point in the cycle.

*9. ***Visit the prospect's management facilities or other "real-world" environment.***

*10. ***Encourage the prospect to visit your referrals projects.***

*11. If you are selling a control service for environmental and industrial control are appropriate for it, consider using flip charts, proposal booklets, a photo presentation booklet during your presentation. It gets people involved and engages the visual sense.

*12. Ask key prospects what they're to accomplish in the area in question for control needs. When you do, you will automatically distinguish yourself from your competition. Don't place too much emphasis on reams of reports, (unless the reports and information proposal packages are formatted for commercial business and associations) color brochures, or elaborate pie charts and regression analyses. Deluging the prospect with information is sometimes a common and costly mistake. As a general rule, prospects will have a hard time forming a positive view of anyone or anything when forced into information overload that is not formatted in a professional manner. Some salespeople ignore this and pile the paper on anyway they can.

*13. When you take notes, take notes! Don't take notes so the prospect will think you're taking notes! If your company requires a graph, then draw a professional graph of the building(s) and take proper notes of what you have found on the property. Never approach your prospects with crumple paper, pens, pencils and eligible appearance.

*14. Bear in mind that by introducing price during the interviewing state. You are relieving much of the pressure from the prospect. For many prospects, you will probably be passing along the extremely valuable information that your service cost less than they think.

*15. Remember that you and the company are working with an individual or with a group of individuals, not an institution. You represent your company, yes—but your company isn't making the presentation, you are. Establish a relationship between two people, not ***two corporate entities***. Tell your prospect that you his business, not that the company does.

*16. Find out decisions relating to purchasing company's service have been made. Odds are that the decision about our service will be made in essentially the same way. Specifically, if you learn that the decision has in the past always been made by a committee, find a way to make your presentation directly to the committee. Don't waste your time with a single member of the committee if you can possibly avoid it.

*17. If you and prospect face a **_considerable gap_** in age or in some other aspect of your professional balance—if, for instance, you are a **_Super Star Woman_** in your mid-twenties trying to close a **_"Dyed-In-The-Wool Good Old Boy"_** in his mid-sixties, who can't seem to bring himself to treat you as a professional equal; consider making your presentation with a another team member of your company. Someone who may be able to put your prospect at ease. This **_"escalation"_** technique is also particularly effective when you're dealing with a prospect who needs reassurance that he or she is making the decision.

*18. **_Aim High_**; don't assume you can't make presentation to the top person in an management organization. Even if this person does not make the final decision regarding the service you have to offer, he or she can be a powerful ally. Try starting at the top and eliciting "**_power referrals_**" from the top people in **_your target organization_**.

*19. Be ready for common objections and don't be caught off guard by obstacles that are common in your company's service and product. If you can remember the pass, you'll probably recall that this has happened to you on a number of occasions. More sales than you might imagine are lost when team members are surprised by **_prospect queries_** and comments that should really come as no surprise at all.
And Finally:

*20. **_Keep your promises. Prospects and Customers will remember you_** . . .

A closing thought in mind, of this chapters' "Thrifty, Brave, Clean and Reverent business decisions."

A little boy appeared under the store owner's sign, "**_Puppies For Sale!_**" "**_How much are you going to sell the puppies for?_**" he asked. The store owner replied, "**Anywhere from $30.00 to $50.00.**" *I have $2.37,*" the little boy said. "*Can I please look at them?*"

The store owner smiled and whistled, and out of the kennel came five teeny, tiny balls of fur. One puppy was lagging considerably behind. Immediately the little boy the single out the lagging, limping puppy and said, "*What's wrong with that little dog?*"

The store owner explained that it had no hip socket; it would always be lame. The little boy became excited. "*That is the little puppy that I want to buy.*"

The store owner, "**No, you don't want to buy that little dog. If you really want him, I'll just give him to you.**"

The little boy got quite upset. He looked straight into the store owner's eyes, pointing his finger, and said, "*I don't want you to give him to my. That little dog is worth every bit as much as all the other dogs and I'll pay full price. In fact, I'll give you $2.37 now, $.50 cents a month until I have him paid for.*"

The store owner countered, "**You really don't want to buy this little dog. He is never going to be able to run and jump and play with you like the other puppies.**"

To this, the little boy reach down and rolled up pant leg to reveal a badly twisted, crippled left leg supported by a big metal brace. He looked up at the store owner and softly replied, "*Well, I don't run so well myself, and the little puppy will need someone who understands!*"

Some days in our business life, a little *__pride__* goes a long way. Especially when you need someone who understands you . . . .

CHAPTER 10

GOOD BUSINESS TURN

When people hear the *"A Good Business Turn,"* they almost think of your business. Not that the idea of helping started with the business, because of course it didn't;—the bible story of a *"Samaritan's Good Turn"* is known to millions as are the adventures of *King Arthur's Knights* bringing help to those in distress. But in the modern world of prospective people do associate the words *"Good Business Turn"* with your company.

This is true because since the beginning of your business adventures, every new *"Winner's Circle Team Members"* has proudly accepted the obligation to do a *Good Turn* to someone everyday. It is more than likely, your *Company's Slogan*, is just as *"Be Prepared"* as is the Boy Scouts Of America Motto. together this *"Good Turn"* carries much of the meaning and spirit of the company's *"Oath and Law."*

A *Good Turn* means doing something helpful, but it means more than that. It means doing something extra, beyond what you would do ordinarily.

This takes watchfulness on your part as a *Team Leader Member*. As a *Team Leader Member*, you are expected to be on the lookout for *Good Turn Opportunities*. You can develop that type of *"observation ability,"* just as you can that seeing faint trail signs. along with this ability to recognize *Good Turn Opportunities* will come your *daily check—upon* yourself. *"Have I done a Good Turn yet today?"* Of course, you should not stop at one *Good Turn.* But it often is surprising how much special attention it takes to find that *first one each day . . .*

Clean the slate at work with a good turn by performing the following:

*1. Return anything you've borrowed that's still around your office or home.

*2. Do something about proposal projects that aren't making any progress. Either dump them or get them finished.

*3. Get rid of items that trigger negative memories. Or, eliminate the negative emotions you have in association with the items.

*4. Deal with relationships of customers or prospective buyers. If you've been meaning to call someone to keep the relationship going, do it. Mentally say good-bye to other relationships that haven't been successful to you.

*5. **Forgive others.** Until you let go of anger towards others it tends to dominate your attention and distract you from more important things . . . .

When your creative efforts or good turns that work always:

*1. ***Start off right***. Be certain goals and objectives are clear, and in depth research, product, service and market information are provided.

*2. ***Never look at creative work when you're in a bad mood***. You may discount good promotions and ideas without good reason.

*3. ***Think like the target audience***. It only matters what your target audience thinks, not what you do. Put yourself in their shoes.

*4. ***Read everything at least twice before you comment***. consider the message and now how it is written. Then point out your concern, and ask your prospect to address them.

*5. ***Discuss what needs to change***. Be specific about tone, content, technical issues, vocabulary, and visual to your prospect or current customer . . . .

If you are just doing your job and what the prospect asked you to do, you probably won't get a "***Good Turn Notice***." You have to go the ***extra mile*** and have a positive attitude if people are going to notice you. Here are some simple business ways to get you notice:

*1. Ask for a performance review formally or informally from your:
     [a] *Manager*
     [b] *Sales Manager*

    [c]   *Service Manager*
    [d]   *Current Customer*
    [e]   *Prospect*

*2. Document what you do in informal memos to your:
    [a]   *Manager*
    [b]   *Sales Manager*
    [c]   *Service Manager*
    [d]   *Current Customer*

This will accumulate to quite a file.

*3. An old standby is to come in early and work late. If other team members always see you there, they are going to be impressed.

*4. Ask your:
    [a]   *Manager*
    [b]   *Sales Manager*
    [c]   *Service Manager*

What new skills could help you at your goals.

*5. Volunteer for an extra service or sales project that is close to the heart of your:
    [a]   *Manager*
    [b]   *Sales Manager*
    [c]   *Service Manager*

Doing some research for one of them, will give you the added edge of becoming a "*Winner's Circle Team Leader.*"

Where you passed over for a "Team Leader" promotion? The two most common reasons why some sales and service team members are not promoted to the "*Team Leader Theme,*" are:

*1. You haven't explicitly stated that you are looking to be "*Winner's Circle Team Leader*" for the year.

*2. You are in a department where few sales and service team members are promoted into a *Team Leader Mission.* Tell your supervisor or sales manager and other higher-ups you are looking for a way to be promoted to be *Team Leader* and ask their advice on the best way to obtain it in your territory. If you are in a department from which few have made it to the *Team Leader Teams*, determine where in your company most promotions are made and consider seeking some information from those *Team Leaders.* This will be a *Good Business Turn* for those who made it all the way for the last few years.

Include the following in your ***Good Turn Mission Statement*** to be a *Team Leader:*

*1.   ***Statement of Purpose***: Describe an inspiring purpose that appeals to higher values rather than selfish interest. Include company's responsibility to team members.

*2.   ***Statement of Strategy***: This defines a business domain and explains why it's attractive. It includes the strategic positioning for success.

*3.   ***Statement of Value***: This identifies values that form a link with the purpose and that your company can be proud of it. The values should re-enforce the team member's strategy.

*4.   ***Statement of Behavioral Standards***: Describe clear behavioral standards for the strategy and values.

*5.   ***Statement of Character***: This statement is easy to read and it provides a clear statement of the company's culture.

A *Good Turn* for ***Sales Forecasting*** is the process of organizing and analyzing information in a way that makes it possible to estimate what your sales will be to become a "Winner's Circle Team Member." This document outlines some of the simple methods of forecasting sales by using easy to find data. Books containing simple and sophisticated techniques of forecasting sales can be found in libraries and business oriented seminars and book stores.

If you sell more than ***one type*** of product or service, prepare a separate sales forecast for each service or product group.

There are many sources of information to assist with your sales forecast. Some key sources are:

*1.   Competitors

*2.   Neighboring Businesses, management companies, associations and residents.

*3. Trade Suppliers.
*4. Trade associations and seminars.
*5. Trade Publications
*6. Trade Directories
*7. Statistics

Factors That Can Affect Sales:

External:

Seasons	Family formations	Fashions or Styles
Holidays	Births and Deaths	Population Changes
Special Events	Political Events	Consumer Earnings
Direct Competition	External Labor Events	Weather
Indirect Competition	Productivity Changes	

Internal:

Product changes, style, quality	Sales Motivation Plans
Credit policy changes	Shortages, inventory
Service changes, type, quality	Labor Problems
Price changes	Promotional Effort changes

The Use of Distribution Methods:

Sales forecasting for a New Business, can be provided by the following steps for developing a sales forecast that can be applied to other kinds of service as well.

*Step 1—Develop a customer profile and determine this trends in your company's territory. Make some basic assumptions about the customers or prospects in your target market. Experienced your top Winner's Circle Team Members *good rule of thumb*, that 20% of your customers accounts for 80% of your sales. If you can identify this **20 %**, you can begin to develop a profile of your principal markets.

Sample Customer Profile:

* Young families, parents 25 to 39, middle income, home owners.
* Management Companies and associations.

Determine trends by talking to trade suppliers at some seminars or trade shows about what is selling well and what is not. Check out recent copies of various trade magazines. Search the "***Business Periodicals Index***," that could be found in libraries for articles related to your service that you are selling.

***Step 2**—Established the approximate size and location of your planned servicing area. Use available statistics to determine the general characteristics of this area. Use local sources to determine unique characteristics about your servicing area.

How far will your prospect call to buy service? Where do you intend to distribute or promote your product and service? This is your service area.

Estimating the number of individuals, associations or households can be done with little difficulty using ***Statistics U.S.*** census data. ***Statistics Family Expenditure Survey*** can identify what the average association or household spends on goods and services. Local Status in your area has population forecast. Information on planned construction is available from a variety of sources. Directories like—

*   ***Contact Target Marketing***
*   ***Local Manufacturing directory***
*   ***Yellow Pages can help identify names of Management Associations located in your area.***
*   ***Neighborhood business owners, the local Chamber of Commerce, the Government Agent and the community newspaper of your area. For Instance—"City areas verus County areas selling in your service areas.***

***Step 3**—List and profile competitors. Meet them at a county meeting, trade show or seminars. Analyze your location, customer volumes, traffic patterns, hours of operation (whether they have night routes or not), busy periods, prices, quality of their goods and services, product lines carried, promotional techniques, positioning, proposal booklets and other handouts. If feasible, talk to customers and management associations.

Step 4**—Use your research to estimate your sales on a monthly basis for your first year. The basis for the "Winner's Circle Sales Forecast,***" can be the average monthly sales of a similar-sized competitor's operations who is operating in a similar market. It is recommended that you make adjustments for this year's predicted trend for you in your area. Be sure to reduce figures by a ***Start-up year factor*** of about ***50 %*** a month for the ***"Start-Up Months."*** Consider how well your competition satisfies the needs of potential customers in your service area. Determine how you fit into this posture and what ***niche*** you plan to fill. Will you offer a better technician, convenience, a better price, later hours, better quality, better service?

   Consider Population And Economic Growth In Your Service Area. Using your research, make an educated guess at your service areas. If possible, express this as the number of prospects you can hope to attract. You may want to keep it conservative and reduce your figure by approximately ***15 %***.

   Prepare you ***Winner's Circle Sales Estimates*** month by month. Be sure to assess how seasonal your business is and consider your ***Start Up Months***.

   When forecasting for an existing customer base, it is important to understand your sales revenues from the same month in the previous year. You need to make a good base for predicting sales for the month in the succeeding year. For example, if the trend forecasters in the economy and company predict a general growth of ***04 %*** for the next year, it will be entirely acceptable for you to show each month's projected ales at ***04 %*** higher than your actual ***Winner's Circle Sales*** the previous year.

   Credible forecast can come from those who have the actual customer contact. Get with the ***Winner's Circle Sales Member or Team or Service Manager*** most closely associated with a particular product line, service, · market or territory to give their base estimates. Experience has proven the grass roots forecast can be surprisingly accurate.

   The Winner's Circle Sales Forecasting and the Business Plan can be summarize by the data after it has been reviewed and revised. The summary will form a part of your business plan. The ***Winner's Circle Sales Forecast*** for the first year should be monthly, while the forecast for the next two years could be expressed as a ***quarterly figure***. Get a second opinion. Have the Winner's Circle Sales Forecast checked by a sales manager who is familiar with your line of selling. Show them the factors you have considered and explain why you think the figures are realistic.

   Your skills at Winner's Circle Sales Forecasting will improve with experience particularly if you treat it as a ***"Live Super Star"*** forecast. Look over your Star Forecast monthly, insert your actuals, and revise the Winner's Circle Forecast if you any significant discrepancy that cannot be explained in terms of a ***one-time only situation***. In this procedure, your ***Winner's Circle Sales Forecasting Technique*** will instantaneously improve and your ***Winner's Circle Sales Forecast*** will become increasingly legitimate for your company.

Here are ***Three Keys*** to effective ***Quality Sales Management*** programs for you to predict your Winner's Circle Sales and Team Members forecasting.

*1.   They will ***customize*** their programs to your specific situation. There descriptions of the successes of others will not cover the small key changes which often make a deference in culture, morale, and procedures. More than likely, they will not clone someone else's programs.

*2.   They will tie their programs to your vision. Your team will have a strategic objective and your the team's strategies will be accepted by the implement of the quality vision.

*3.   Your ***Sales Manager*** will state out carefully. Initial projects will be simple and easy to achieve. Their programs will build successful momentum for your programs. If you start in an unfocused way with unmanageable projects, the sales manager will be their to help you with the frustrated and disillusions.

When you meet a prospect, you can't expect to remember their names with one mention you may have barely heard. So first make sure that you hear it. Try to repeat their names and use it in conversation. Associate their names with some ***feature and benefit*** of their ***face*** that will remind you of their name when you see them. If you try this and don't see improvement, get their business card or write their name down. Then you can study it at your leisure.

Here are some "***Brainstorming Techniques***" that can help you communicate.

*1.   ***Formulate The Problem***. Do this in a broad, general way. For instance, instead of stating the problem as "***fixing poor communication***," it would be stated as "***facilitating great communication and feedback in a company's structure***.

*2.   ***Create a fictitious problem***. Have the group create a fictitious problem with parallels to the real problem. For instance, the real problem might be how to coordinate the activities of multi-disciplinary teams; the fictitious problems could be how does one get a pile of rocks to sing a tune!

*3. *__Generate options__*. Get the team to list all possible causes for the fictitious problem. Because the problem is fictitious, the team is less inhibited in coming up with unorthodox reasons. The team is also entertained by their humorous responses, which also tends to loosen you up.

Getting through their objections or excuses, can be fixed with a good turn. There are *__two basic types of objections: (1) Sincere Objections__* and *__(2) Excuses:__*

A *__Sincere Objection__* is a valid point you need to address. An *__excuse__*, on the other hand, is aimed at concealing the true concern is.

Team members need to be able to tell the difference. Overcoming excuses is a *__two-art__* process. Many prospects refuse to open themselves up to reveal true concerns. Here are some *__Prospective__* examples of what they might say:

*   *__"I wasn't planning on buying today,"__* which might really mean,
*   *__"I'm not convinced that this is the right service,"__* or
*   *__"I don't like your terms,"__* or any of a dozen other valid concerns.

Your job is to ignore this brush-off and ask questions to uncover the __true reason__ for the resistance. For example:

__"I'm just looking,"__ you might respond: *__"That's the best way to familiarize yourself with our wide selection of service. Is there anything I can help you find?"__*

Customers sometimes make irrational objections that have no basis in fact. In the case, ask them to explain:

*   *__"I'm not sure I understand, Mr. Smith. Could you elaborate?"__* This approach usually prompts prospects to rethink their objections and take a more reasonable stance. Objections and excuses are both used to delay sales. Be aware of the difference. Then face them head on and move forward with the sales.

CHAPTER 11

NAILING THE OPENER

Paul Bunyan, Legend, and Folklore. *Paul Bunyan,* a legendary hero of lumber camps of the **_American Northwest_**. Endowed with enormous **_strength, vision, speed, humor,_** and **_cunning_**. Paul Bunyan has become the basis of saga suited to the vastness of the North American continent. According to the legend, Paul Bunyan and his giant blue ox, **_Babe_**, left an indelible mark on the landscape of America. Paul Bunyan created **_Puget Sound_**, the **_Grand Canyon_** and the **_Black Hills_**, and Babe could haul an entire forest at one time. Some authorities find a French-Canadian origin for this **_folklore_**; others believed that the tale was a fabrication of a logging company during the early 20th century. Still others consider the legend of Paul Bunyan as an **_European_** import, elements of which were later magnified. All agree that the fusion of bigness with the "**_tall story_**" is a legend peculiarly (uncommon) American. This legend circulated through the logging camps of **_Michigan, Wisconsin,_** and **_Minnesota_**, where the rugged loggers first heard and then retold the **_Paul Bunyan_** fables, adding local or personal or ancestral embellishments. Some of the stories of Paul Bunyan were published be **_James Mac Gillivary_** in the **_Detroit News—Tribune_** on July 24, 1910. **_W. B. Laughead_** adapted them to a series of pamphlets advertising the "**_Red Lumber Company._**" Through these mean, the stories of **_Paul Bunyan_** founded a growing audience. The "**_Stories_**" have been rewritten by many popular writers for readers of all ages. For years, **_Folklore_**, general terms for verbal, spiritual, and material aspects of any culture that are transmitted orally, by observation and by imitation. People who shared a culture in occupations, inventions, language, ethnicity, age, or geographical location as been passed from one generation to another. Some companies to whom you are working with or for was noted as the ***First U.S. Patent*** ever to be awarded for their product or service. Do you think Paul Bunyan once first work with your company?

Chances are that after you read this sentence, you'll decide whether to read the rest of this about "***Nailing The Opener***." You've just proved how important the first sentence of a sales letter is.

Sales Letters are like ***advertisements*** . . . . It is often the headline in the ***ad*** that grabs the ***reader's attention***, drawing the prospect into the rest of the message. That is precisely what the first sentence of a sales letter should—***make that must-do***.

Getting your letter to stand out from all the others is ***Goal No. 1***. Begin with something that is little different from the other letters that cross your prospect's desk. Most Team Leaders state letters essentially the same way:

*1.   With an explanation—often almost a defense.
*2.   ***Example***: I want to take the opportunity to explain our "***Partnership for Protection Plan***," program.
*3.   To make your letter stand out, you should get to the point immediately with:
         **   Our program is a full "***Service and Product Repair***" warranty.

*4.   In a cover letter that accompanies sales literature, don't start with:
         **   Enclosed is the information you requested about . . . .

*5.   That is like starting an in-person call with the statement:
         **   ***I'm here to make a sales call***."

*6.   More effective is an opening statement about company's service or products you are using—better yet, about how or why the customer is going to benefit from it.
         **   "This means to you that (***your company's name***) is responsible for all future service and repairs."

The best first sentence often is found buried somewhere in the body of the letter. Take a good look through some of your recent correspondence and you will probably find a *one-sentence, benefit-oriented "<u>headline</u>"* that says it all; *promote it to front-line status.*

The same principle applies when writing a follow-up letter to a phone call on a meeting. Never start the with "*<u>Thank you</u>*." The reader who see an opener like "*Thank you for meeting with me,*" or "*Thank you for your time on the phone the other day,*" will more than likely tend to dismiss the rest of the letter, because the prospect assumes you have nothing more to say than that.

Instead, make a *<u>knowledgeable</u>* and *<u>empathetic</u>* statement, and make it from the customer's point of view.

*1.   "*Achieving sales goals in a competitive environment such as your can't be left to chance.*"

*2.   "*Our systems represents an <u>Integrated Management</u> approach for the protection of the business and structures.*"

*3.   "*Our company (name) would like to offer our services and request the opportunity to <u>bid</u> on any service projects you may in your area. Our hopes is that after considering our advantages of dealing with one of the top companies, who will make a positive decision to allow us to service product and protect your costly investments.*

The best opening sentences do more than grab attention; they draw the prospects into the letter. When you are making a statement, be sure it ties in with what you are selling. And if you ask a question, be sure the answer the plays in your favor. When protection is needed, customers ask someone with experience to do the job. Chances are high the answer will be "*<u>yes</u>*." The keys to successful letter writing are getting the prospect and customer's attention and giving them a reason to read the rest of the letter. If you avoid typical openers and get straight to how the *<u>customer's benefits</u>*, your letters will stand apart from the others, dramatically increasing chances of communicating your sales message.

<u>OPENING SHOTS</u>:

*   *STRAIGHT SALE'S LETTER USING CUSTOMER-ORIENTED STATEMENT . . .*

    *   When Executive Business named "most likely to succeed," there was only one thing left for you to do:

     * *Tell them how (your company) can help turn "likely" into "certain."*

* *TO GET AN APPOINTMENT WHEN PROSPECT WON'T RETURN PHONE CALLS; USE A QUESTION:*
> * "You obviously recognize the benefits of our products and service for your business. Won't you take a closer look at ours and imagine reaching a new goal for sales of sales of your products in your warehouse will be with our service program."

* *APOLOGY LETTER USING EMPATHY AND HUMILITY WITH CUSTOMER-ORIENTED STATEMENT AND QUESTION:*
> * "Your disappointment at how your service and product account has been handled is understandable, especially in light of your company's reputation for excellence. Since there is no good excuse for our company (<u>name</u>) poor performance, may I make it up to you with this offer?"

* *STRAIGHT SALES LETTER USING CUSTOMER-ORIENTED BENEFIT STATEMENT:*
> * "Reliable service in your business is more than just a phrase; it's the difference between success and failure. That is why you need a service and product company that really delivers."

* *FOLLOW-UP AFTER MEETING, USING BENEFIT STATEMENT, GETTING TIGHT TO THE POINT AND AVOIDING "THANK YOU" IN THE FIRST PARAGRAPH:*

*Dear _____,

It has been my pleasure to work with you to provide a solution for your service and product needs. I am pleased that you selected our company, (<u>name</u>), and that we were able to demonstrate the professionalism that our company prides itself upon.

To continue to be of service, I am available for any other requirements you might have. If you have a problem or comment on any of our company's service, please do not hesitate to contact me.

Thank you for calling (Company's name)!
My phone number is _____.
Sincerely,

Whatever Happen To he Plain, Ordinary Salesperson? If you look at business cards today, there are not too many that just have the title of "***Salesperson***." Today, with your company, they are most likely known as "***Associated***," "_____ ***Specialist***," "***Commercial/Residential Specialist***," "_____ ***Inspector***," "***Customer Coordinator***," and a lot of other titles that used to be categorized under simple "***sales***."

Nobody just ask for an order anymore; now there are selling systems, such as "***Pest Control Elimination System Service***, or ***Insurance Protection System Service***." They tell you that you have to do a lot of things to become a successful "***Super Star Salesperson.***" Things like *qualifying, probing, listening, presenting, refocusing, planning, and managing your time.*

Then there are proposal books that tell you can't just find a need and ask the customer to buy. They talk about asking all sorts of questions such as ***open, closed, discovery, standard tie-down, inverted tie-down, clarifying and opinion.*** Then of course, you have to learn to close. And according to a lot of these proposal books, tapes, and systems, it's not easy either. There's the "***Ben Franklin Close, Alternative Close, the Test and Trial Close, the Crash and Burn Close, the Sharp Angle Close, the If-I-Could-Would-You Close, and that's just the beginning closes.***"

Now, guess what? Your customer are street-wise—they know the closes and the tricks. If you think about all the systems and the programs on selling, the underlying assumption beneath this multitude of techniques is that you're selling the customer something they don't want to hear about. This isn't what selling is all about!

You have to establish a ***need*** first. Then fill it. That is the basics. Then you have the strength to ask a person to buy and the persistence to ask several times, in creative ways that don't turn a prospect off. You need ***charm and the personality*** to be their friend. If you concentrate on ***selling***, the customer something they want, you won't have to worry about the latest trends in questions, closes, or selling systems.

Selling creatively doesn't mean putting someone else's words in your mouth. Find out what works for you and perfect it. If someone else's selling style doesn't fit your behavioral patterns, you look phony. You need to start to *"sound"* like a *Super Star*. Prospects don't want to be sold—they want to buy.

If you are getting bogged down with *false* complexity and jargon, it might be time to step away from the confusion to remind yourself of what you are really trying to do. Selling takes a little more than knowing your company's products and service. *Persistence and creativity* can increase sales more than any formula ever could.

Knowing how to be motivated by building *Self-Esteem* as an ordinary salesperson, here are five ways to build this *esteem*:

*1. Make prospects feel secure about you. Don't threaten them, keep your promises, and be honest.
*2. Promote group cohesion when you work with a management company. Create a social network where prospects and customers gain support.
*3. Make them feel valuable to your company. Set up meetings where people can report on their latest accomplishments and gain recognition.
*4. Empower prospects and customers. Involved them in decisions that affect them. Show respect for their opinions.
*5. Give prospects and customers unconditional acceptance. Confidence develops originally in young children because they feel unconditionally accepted by parents.

To motivate more effectively, pay attention to what motivation techniques works best for each individual. *Super Stars* and *Top Winner's Circle Performers*, might quickly get tire of routine. *Marginal performers* will probably require more one-on-one interaction to help maintain their focus and attention to detail. *Consistent performers*, or those who make of the backbone of the company's team, will probably require regular support and encouragement.

To recognize each other, encourage the team members to publicly recognize fellow team members for outstanding performances. Schedule an informal awards ceremony where medals, certificates, or a cup of coffee and a doughnut can be presented to each other.

Another idea is sent up a ___12 Marbles Award___, in your own color. Over a course of the year, dispense the marbles as a reward to team members who help each other, or to recognize great performances. At the and of the year, you may ___Lost Your Marbles___ and not make it to the "___Super Star Winner's Circle___, but you should have gained some new ones. So, try it all out, or you may never know you have inside your ___motivational Self-Esteem___.

Let us think now, on how to get more ___Motivational Perspective___. If you are feeling terrible about your job situation and would like to leave, try this. Tell yourself that you are leaving in two weeks, and then see if the same little things bother you. By pretending you are leaving, you get a more balance view of the situation that allows you to rise above petty problems. Give yourself some intellectual detachment. Quit worrying about everything that isn't fair and things that you have no control over. And ___don't put unrealistic expectations on yourself___.

Good selling involves ___asking the right questions and listening to the answers.___ Here are ___six___ tips that you can ask for more effective sales questions:

*1. Does the questions challenge the prospect to think in a new way about the company's product, system or service?

*2. Does the question make you seem more knowledgeable than competitors about the company's product, system, or service?

*3. Does the question build rapport by having a prospect share something they are proud of?

*4. Does the question generate a response the prospect never thought of before the product, system, or service was develop?

*5. Does the question relate directly to the situation your prospect is in, such as your service?

*6. Does the question give you information that will allow you to make the product, system, or service sale better?

Before you make a cold—call, gather as much information about the product, system, and service as you can. It should be:

*1. Type of product, system, or service the prospect management company provides to its' customers.

*2. Methods used to sell the product and the service.
*3. History of the company and the product, system and service.
*4. Names of the prospect's customers.
*5. Names of the decision makes within the management company and the customers.
*6. Research on the prospect's management industry.

If you want the sale, ask for it! History has shown that one of the big mistakes made team members who want the sales is not asking for it. What is recommended is that when you ask for the sale, show *__*Enthusiasm* and__ *__*Energy__*—This applies whether your are down on sales you want, or you sold some but not enough to the "___Winner's Circle___."

CHAPTER 12

THERE IS A DIFFERENCE!

A *theologian* and *astronomer* were talking together one day. The astronomer said that after reading widely in the field of religion, he had concluded that all religion could be summed up in a single phrase.

"*Do unto others as you would have them do unto you,*" he said, with a bit of smugness, knowing that his field is so much more complex.

After a brief pause, the theologian replied that after reading widley in the area of astronomy, he had concluded that all of it could be summed up in a single phrase also.

"*Oh, and what is that?*" the astronomer inquired.

"*Twinkle, twinkle, little star, how I wonder what you are!*" replied the theologian. "*There Is A Difference!*"

The right name, an attractive company sign on your vehicle, the correct uniform will help you to build *company spirit*. But, after all, they are only things. Their value depends on the life you put into them.

Company Symbols means nothing if it is just something tucked away in a dark trunk of your vehicle. Their value depends on the life you put into them. The uniform has no meaning to the team members if it is something to wear.

It's the same will all the other things you just talked about. Without life, they're without meaning.

The *company symbols* takes on meaning when it is taken along on every job. When it is shown outside their business, when it shown as its' waves from the top of the building, your *company's names has "conquered."* The uniform has meaning when the whole technical team does things together in that uniform. The branch, region, and division sales managers picks up meaning when they give it to pep up the *Super Stars Teams* for a company branch and region meetings. Company songs when you use it to pull yourselves through the last mile of the twelve month selling adventure for the _**Super Stars Winner's Circle**_.

You as the _**Super Star Leader**_ have a great responsibility. Your guiding spirit will put life into selling, meetings and winner circles. Your _**enthusiasm**_ will make _**Company Spirit**_ grow . . . . "_**There is a Difference!**_"

What does it take to be a _**Super Star Leader**_? A Super Star leader must have:

* _**Dreams, visions**_, and _**big ideas**_ that can be shared with others.
* A remarkable capacity to focus single-mindedly on what it takes to accomplish the dream.
* The ability to tirelessly seek the involvement of others in your vision. You as a _**Super Star,**_ generally not interested in showing off your skills or knowledge. You do take part and support others who get involved with the goal.

Developing your intuition make decision and have a gut feeling about what the correct course of action is, it's usually worthwhile to rely on it. If you're unsure about your _**intuition, write down your best guesses**_ in a situation and wait until later events unfold. As you see that your intuition has a high hit rate, you'll be more comfortable using.

**Super Star Team Leaders** contribute 20% of the success of most companies. Followers contribute the other _**80 %**_. But, followers get none of the glory. To be a good _**Super Star Team Leader**_, support the your "_**followers**_."

*1. Be an advocate for their ideas to higher management.
*2. Obtain the resources the team needs to achieve its goals.
*3. Reduce productivity road blocks, such as interruptions.
*4. _**Encourage Self-management.**_
*5. Give team members who understand the problem the responsibility for solving it.
*6. Involve followers in decisions that directly affect them, such as selling commercial products and services.
*7. Give public recognition to followers for their contributions.

Your _**voice or phonation**_, is the sound produce by the expiration of air through vibrating vocal cords. Boca is defined in terms of _**pitch, quality,**_ *and* *intensity, or* *loudness*. Optimum pitch, which means the most appropriate pitch of speaking when proposing a produce or service and system, varies with each individual team member. Both optimum pitch and range of pitch are fundamentally determined by the *length* and *mass* of the vocal cords. Within these limits, pitch maybe varied by changing the combination of *air pressure* and *tension* of the vocal cords. This combination determines the frequency which the vocal cords vibrate. The greater the frequency of vibration, the higher the pitch.

Another aspect of voice is *Resonance*. After voice is produced, it is resonated in the *chest, throat, and cavities* of the month. The quality of the voice is determined by resonance and the manner in which the vocal cords vibrate. Intensity is controlled by resonance and by the strength of the vibrations of the vocal cords.

Articulation refers to the speech sounds that are produced to form the words of language. The articulating mechanism comprises the *lips, tongue, teeth, jaw, and palate*. Speech is articulated by interrupting or shaping both the vocalized and unvocalized air stream through movement of the *tongue, lips, lower jaw, and soft palate*. The teeth are used to produce some specific speech sounds.

So, watch how you present your proposal and pointing out the areas of interest to the customer or client.

When presenting a letter explaining that *"There is a Difference,"* put a package together with this introduction letter:

_____, 2010

_____

_____

_____,(Your state), (zip code)

Dear _____,

The purpose of this information package is to:
*Provide cost information per your at the _____
_____ properties.
*Provide all preliminary information about the service, product, or our system process.
*Quality (*Company Name*) as the "**Right**" choice.

As you progress through the decision process on such a major issue as _____ protection, it will be important for you to be able to accurately compare service, product, or system options, cost and liabilities.

"THERE IS A DIFFERENCE"

To accomplish such comparisons, the importance of accurate communication and ability to clarify differences and similarities will command a high priority. At anytime during this process that you need additional information or questions answered; we stand prepared to meet with you or to field your questions via telephone conversations.

This proposal package will outline the procedures and your investment cost for the service we provide, as well as guarantee program renewable for the life of the (**items or structure**).

Upon review of this proposal package, I am confident you agree that:

"THERE IS A DIFFERENCE."

Thank you for calling on (**Your Company's Name**)
Sincerely,

_____
name

_____
Your position as a specialist

There are four "*Principles For Setting Your Stretch Goals.*"

THERE IS A DIFFERENCE!

*1. *The Principle Of Aspiration*: "Who do you want to be?"* You each have personal aspirations and a desire to excel. Your aspirations are often embedded in the work that you do in group team, management companies and communities. For example, you want to be part of the "*Winner's Circle Team*, that is known for the highest quality or outstanding service. Yet, often times, the bar of excellence is too low to release the collective aspiration of the team or to inspire teams to bring their whole selves to work.

The role of the coach (team leader) is to inspire teams to raise the bar of excellence. Creating a stretch goal is one way to release the collective aspirations of the team and inspire extraordinary levels of commitment from the individual. The examples of the *Apollo Moon* landing and *3M bear this out.*

*2.   *The Principle Of Lever*: *"How do you apply your resources so they can make the biggest difference?"* One of the defining characteristics of a *stretch goal* is that something, while exciting, seems difficult or almost impossible to achieve. As mentioned, for the goal to be a *stretch*, it should create a deliberate mismatch between the teams aspirations and ambitions and its' present and knowledge and resources. This means that to achieve the goal, your team needs to learn to get more out of what you have. One of the functions of the coach (team leader) is to help teams to do just that. This not only applies to deriving more from material resources but to tapping the hidden reserve of creativity and effectiveness that is usually available in any team. When you create a deliberate mismatch between what needs to be achieved and what teams already think and know, you force teams to think outside the box and to move beyond the limits of your existing *paradigms*.

*3.   *The Principle Of Convergence*: *"What can you create together?"* There is an old Greek saying: *"Alone we can be great, together we can be greater."* Stretch goals allow teams to come together to create something larger than themselves. The coach's (team leader) role is often to act as a "*Steward*" in the process of convergence. It helps if the teams is a natural team with a common calling, like wanting to design and implement a learning approach rather than a bureaucratic one. It also helps if each team member has something to contribute that makes the more powerful.

*4.   *The Principle Of Concentration*: *"What are one or two goals to focus on?* A book put out by *Peter Drucker—The Effective Executive*—said that *"The signal most important principle of human effectiveness is concentration. Experience shows that there need to be one or two long-term, inspirational goals that become navigation post to the future and that ensure different people and departments are focused on the same thing."* The principle of concentration also is applied to concentrating resources on *key strategic goals* where you can have the most impact. Small teams sometimes cannot hold their focus on goals that too big or too long. Your **_Team Leader Coach_** can help by getting the team focused on measurable objectives that can be done in weeks, not months.

There are four more ways to make a "**_Decision_**" in managing your sales as a "**_Winner's Circle Super Star._**" They are: **_Tell, Sell, Consult, and Consensus_**.

*1. **_Telling_** is the old-fashioned way. You tell prospects what is the decisions and that's that . . . .
*2. **_Selling_** is starting with your idea and trying to convince prospects to accept it and co-operate.
*3. **_Consulting_** involves the prospects affected under you, but it reserves the final decision for yourself.
*4. **_Consensus_** gets true impute from customers and prospects, and the decision is made as a **_Super Star Team Member_**. This technique is sometimes slower in the short term, but it's often faster when it comes to getting the service implemented. Once the decision is made, the prospects involved are already on board and want to make it work.

Your **_Career Skills_** that you can work on, is **_Practice, Develop, and Aim_**.

*1. **_Practice_** accomplishing more tasks in a given amount of time. Your **_quantity_** and **_quality_** level of results are very direct measures of yourself discipline.
*2. **_Develop_** more control over your day. Plan your schedule the night before or first thing in the morning, and follow your plan. Concentrate on making things go the way you want more often, reducing that chaotic feeling, and positioning yourself to handle obstacles and ambiguous situations.
*3. **_Aim_** more directly towards your goals, and your interim objectives leading up to these goals.

And finally in this chapter, there are "*The __10__ Most Powerful Types Of Sales Stories:*

*1. __Introductory Stories__. Tells about who you are, how you've help others.

*2. __Attention—Grabbing Stories__. Gets people interested in listening.

*3. __Product Information Stories__. Instead of *laundry-listing features and benefits* of your company's product or services, you use this information a fascinating story.

*4. __Stories Overcome Fear__. Illustrates how others experienced the same fears there listeners has and how they later learned they don't need to worry after all.

*5. __Money Stories__. Give examples of how they can afford your product/service. Shows how they will save money.

*6. __Improved Productivity Stories__. Shows how your product/service helped others increase their efficiency, output, sales, and decreased errors, trouble, hassles, and flaws.

*7. __Ego Enhancement Stories__. Shows how owning and using your product/service has increased other customers' self-confidence, pride, self-esteem.

*8. __Family Togetherness Stories__. Shows how your product/ service has brought families closer together.

*9. __Security Stories__. Reveals how doing business with you and your company has given people, *__peace of mind, emotional,__ and __financial security__*.

*10. __Closing Stories__. Wraps up the commitment and gets the sale !!!!!!!!

CHAPTER 13

HUMANISM AND INTEGRITY

*"Fourscore and seven years ago, our fathers brought forth
on this continent, a new nation, conceived in Liberty, and
dedicted to the proposition that all men are created equal."*

On this day, November 19, 1863, United States President Abraham Lincoln made a famous speech known as the ***Gettysburg Address***. His speech was the start of a dedication of ***Humanism and Integrity*** during a time of a great Civil War.

Humanism, in philosophy, attitude that emphasizes the dignity and worth of the individual. A basic premise of humanism is that people are rational beings who possess within themselves the capacity for ***truth and goodness***. The term ***humanism*** is most often used to describe a literary and cultural movement that spread through western Europe in the 14th and 15th centuries. The Renaissance revival of Greek and Roman studies emphasized the value of the classics for their own sake, rather than for their relevance.

Integrity, an incorporation of desparate ethnic or religious elements of the population into a unified society, providing equuality of opportunity for all members of that society. In such a society, an individual's attainment of aneducation, access to any public or private facility, opportunity for employment, and ownership of property are neither denied nor limited by reason of race, religion, or national origin. In the country that we live in, complete integration is a steadfast adherence to a strict moral or ethical code. It is a soundness and completeness of unity.

As the 16th President of the United States, Abraham Lincoln helped keep the American Union together during the Civil War. He was remembered for his honesty, compassion, and strength of character. Lecoln remains one of the most respected presidents in American History.

The "***Silent Journey***." The mysteries of nature are elusive, concealed from view. The miraculous interwoven web of nature dances before our eyes each day, yet remains somehow hidden. Until we stop, ***Listen, Watch, And Wait.***

What is Stress Management ? In our business ***Stress*** occurs when we have to write a report, bid for commercial management's service, and controlling their services with a product. *stress* also occurs when there is an imbalance between the demands of our lives and the resources we have to deal with those demands. An imbalance may happen when there are changes in our lives such as making it to the ***Super Star Winner's Circle***. It's not the changes themselves, but our ***reaction*** to those changes or events that determines if we feel stressed.

The first step to ***management stress*** is to identify your ***"Stressors."*** Those are those things that are making you react. Stressors may not only be events that cause you to feel sad, fightened, anxious or happy. You can cause stress through ***thoughts, feelings, and expectations***. Look at the following list. Which cause you stress? Can you think of the other stressors?

*Not enough time	**Extra responsibility*
*Unexpected change	**Personality clashes*
*Family problems	**Money difficulties*

Instead of letting stress control you, ***Take Action*** !!!!!! Here are "***Seven Stress Management Solutions*** to start you on the right path.

*1. ***Manage Your Time***—The solution of running out of time is to take time to plan and organize.
  *   Make a realistic "***to do***" list and priortize. Keep in mind that everything may not get done and that there is always another day.
  *   Get a personal organizer and use it.
  *   Break down task into bite-sized chunks.
  *   Consolidate similar trips and errands.
  *   Delegate as much as possible.
  *   Write agendas for meetings and keep people on track.

*2. ___Build Endurance With Exercise___—Exercise reduces tension and a strong body is better able to handle stress.

   * Choose an aerobic exercise you like. Do it for 20-30 minutes, 3-4 times a week.
   * Take **stretch breaks** at work—a great tension reliever.
   * Walks are an easy way to get exercise and relax.

*3. ___Think Positively___—The expectations and beliefs we hold are sometimes expressed to ourselves as ___self-talk___. Positive self-talk such as "___I can meet this challenge___," or "___I'm in control___," can act as a shield against stress.

   * ___Negative Self-Talk___ **is** stress producing. Thoughts such as "___I can't___" or "___I have to be perfect,___" only make matters worse. Being aware of comments to yourself increases your feelings of self-control and self-confidence.
   * ___Be Prepared___. Mentally rehearse a stressful situations; gather any resources you'll need.

THOUGHT PATTERNS:

	Negative
___Event___ . . .	*You make a mistake at work.*
___Stress Thought___ . . .	*"I just can't do this." "I have failed."*
___Stress Reaction___ . . .	*Sadness, low self-esteem.*

"INSTEAD TRY"

	Positive
___Event___ . . .	*You make a mistake at work.*
___Empowering Thought___ . . .	*"What can I do to improve?" How can I avoid doing this again?"*
___Reaction___ . . .	*Feeling of mastery and self-confidence.*

*4. ___Breaking The Tension Cycle___—When you feel tense, close your eyes and remember to breathe deeply.

   * Get away from it all. Exercise, read a meaningful quote or go out for lunch or dinner.

* Take laughter breaks with friends or fellow workers. you deserve good, healthy fun. Collect jokes.
* Walk away from stressful situation. A few minutes away can help reduce tension and stress.

*5. **_Balance Work & Family_**.—When you feel overwhelmed use these suggestions to get back in control:

* **_Set Limits_**—Learn to say "No." Practice the **_Rule of 2 + 1 + 1._** begin with **_2_** positives, "I enjoy working on this project and I enjoy working with you." The **_1_** negative, "But I can't stay tonight." End with **_1_** more positive, "I can do this first thing in the morning."
* **_Be Brief_**—The longer you talk, the closer you are to giving in.
* **_Balance At Home_**—Cook in large quantities and freeze separate meals.
* Give yourself enough time to shift from one role to another. Use you commute time to get ready for your nest role.
* Established daily and weekly routines for household chores. Share responsibilities.
* Schedule special time with the family members.
* Plan for the unexpected, such as keeping and extra set of car keys around for emergencies.

*6. **_Build A Support Team System_**—No man or woman is an island.

* Each out to others—build a strong network of people at work, home and in your neighborhood whom you are for and who cares are about you.
* Develop relationships and friendships with people you trust.
* Ventilate feelings before they build up. No one knows how you feel unless you tell them. Releasing negative feelings makes room for positive energy.

*7. **_Communicate Effectively-Sending The Message: Receiving The Message:_**

* Organize your message.

* Establish eye contact
* Use "I" statements.
* "When Listen for the whole this happens, I feel . . . ." message, content, feelings and meaning.
* Do not judge or name call
* Check out if you under-stood the message by repeating or summarizing what you thought you heard.
* Be ready to receive feedback
* "You're saying that you feel . . . ."

Use the **_Action Plan_** below write down your ideas on how you can be more effectively deal with stress.

*1.   One thing I will start doing to better handle the everyday stresses of life is:_____

      _____

*2.   I will remind myself to do this by:_____

      _____

*3.   One thing I will start doing to build my endurance to handle stress is: _____

      _____

*4.   I will remind myself to do this by: _____

      _____

Here are **_52 Proven Stress Reducers_** that can make a better life with the everyday stress:

*1.   Get up fifteen minutes earlier in the morning. The inevitable morning mishaps will be less stressful.
*2.   Prepare for the morning the evening before. Set the breakfast table, make lunches, put out the clothes you plan to wear, etc.
*3.   Don't rely on your memory. Write down appointments times, when to pick up the laundry, when library books are due, etc. {**_And Old Chinese Proverb—"The palest ink is better that the most retentive memory."_**
*4.   Doing nothing which, after being done, leads you to tell a **_lie_**.
*5.   Make duplicates of all keys. Bury a house key in a secret spot in the garden and carry a duplicate car key in your wallet, apart from your key ring.

*6. Practice preventive maintenance. Your car, appliances, home and relationships will be less likely to breakdown/fall apart *"at the worst possible moment."*

*7. **Be prepared to wait.** A paperback can make a wait in a post office line almost pleasant.

*8. Procrastination is stressful. Whatever you want to do tomorrow, do today; whatever you want to do today, do it **_now_**.

*9. Plan ahead. don't let the gas tank get below one-quarter full; keep a well-stocked emergency shelf of home staples; don't wait until you're down to your last bus token or postage stamps to more, etc.

*10. Don't put with something that work right. If your alarm clock, wallet, shoe laces, windshield wipers, whatever are a constant aggravation; get them fixed or get new ones.

*11. Allow 15 minutes of extra time to get to appointments. Plan to arrive at an airport two hours before domestic departures.

*12. Eliminate (or restrict) the amount of caffeine in your diet.

*13. Always set contingency plans, *"**_just in case_**."* "If for some reason either of us is delayed, here's what we'll do . . . ." Or, "If we get split up in the shopping center, here's where we'll meet."

*14. Relax your standards. The world will not end if the grass doesn't mowed this weekend.

*15. **_Pollyanna—Power_** !!!! For everyone thing that goes wrong, there are probably 10 or 50 or 100 blessings. Count them !!!!

*16. *Ask questions.* Taking a few moments to repeat back directions, what someone expects you; etc., can save hours. *The old—"the hurried I go, the behinder I get" idea.*

*17. *Say "No . . ."* Saying "no" to extra projects; social activities, and invitations you know you don't have the time or energy for takes practices, self-respect, and a belief that everyone, everyday, needs quiet time to relax and be alone.

*18. *Unplug your phone.* Want to take a long bath, meditate, sleep, or read with interruptions? Drum up the courage to temporally disconnect. The possibly of there being a terrible emergency in the next hour or so is almost nil. Or use an answering machine.

*19. *Simplify, simplify, simplify* . . . .

*20. *Turn needs into preferences.* Our basic physical needs translate into food, water, and keeping warm. Everything else is a preference. Don't get attached to preferences.

*21. Get up and stretch periodically if your job requires that you sit for extended periods.

*22. **Make friends with nonworriers.** Nothing can get you into the habit or worrying faster than associating with **chronic worrywarts**.

*23. **Wear Earplugs**. If you need to find quiet at home, pop in some earplugs.

*24. **Get enough sleep.** If necessary, use an alarm clock to remind you to go to bed.

*25. **Create order out of chaos.** Organized your home and workspace so that you always know exactly where things are. Put things away where they belong and you won't have to through the stress of losing things.

*26. **When feeling stressed, most people tend to breathe in short, shallow breaths.** When you breathe like this, stale air is not expelled, oxidation of the tissues is incomplete and muscle tension frequently results. Check your breathing throughout the day and before, during and after high pressure situations. If you find your stomach muscles are knotted and your breathing shallow, relax all your muscles and take several deep, slow breaths. Note how, when you're relaxed, both your abdomen and chest expand when you breaths.

*27. Writing your thoughts and feeling (in a journal, or a paper to be thrown away) can help you clarify things and can give you a renewed perspective.

*28. **Try following _Yoga_ technique** whenever you feel the need to relax. Inhale deeply through your nose to the count of eight. Then with lips puckered, exhale very slowly through your mouth to the count of fifteen or for as long as you can. Concentrate on the long sighing sound and feel the tension dissolve. Repeat **_Ten Times_** !!!!

*29. **Inoculate yourself against a feared event.** Examples; before speaking in public, take time to go over every part of the experience in your mind. Imagine what you'll wear, what the audience will look like, how you will present your talk, what the questions will be and how you will answer them, etc. Visualize the experience the way you would have to be. When the time comes to make the actual presentation; it will be an **_"old hat"_** and much of your anxiety will have fled.

*30. When the stress of having to get a job done gets in the way of getting the job done, diversion—a—voluntary change in activity and/or environment—maybe just what you need.

*31. **Talk it out . . .** Discussing your problem with a trusted friend can help clear your mind of confusion so you can concentrate on problem solving.

*32. One of the obvious ways to avoid unnecessary stress is to select and environment (work, home, leisure) which is in line with your personal needs and desires. If you hate desk jobs, don't accept a job which require that you sit at a desk all day. If you hate to talk politics, don't associate with people who love to talk politics, etc.

*33. **Learn to live one day at a time.**

*34. **Everyday, do something you really enjoy.**

*35. **Add an once of love to everything you do.**

*36. **Take a hot bath or shower (or cool one in the summer time) to relieve tension.**

*37. **Do something for somebody else.**

*38. **Do something that will improve your appearance.**
Looking better can help you feel better and avoid tattoos, and dying of the hair like Dennis Rodman.

*39. Focus on understanding rather than on being understood; on loving rather being loved.

*40. **Schedule a realistic day.** Avoid the tendency to schedule back-to-appointments. Allow time between appointments for a breathing spell.

*41. **Become more flexible.** Some things are not worth doing perfectly and some issues are well to compromise upon. *42. Eliminate destructive self-talk. **"I'm too old to . . . , or I'm too fat to . . . ,"** etc.

*43. **Use your weekend time for a change pace.** If your work week is slow and patterned, make sure there is action and time for spontaneity built into your weekends. If your work is fast-paced and full of people and deadlines, seek peace and solitude during your days off. Feel as if you aren't accomplishing at work? Tackle a job on the weekend which you can finish to your satisfaction.

*44. **"Worry about the pennies and the dollars will take of themselves."** That's another way of saying; take care of the todays as best you can and the yesterdays and tomorrow's will take care of themselves.

*45. ***Do one thing at a time.*** When you are with someone. be with that person and with with no one else. When you are busy with a project, concentrate on doing that project and forget about everything else you have to have to do.

*46. ***Allow yourself time-everyday-for privacy, quiet, and introspection.***

*47. If an especially unpleasant task faces you, do it early in the day and get it over with; then the rest of your day will be free of anxiety.

*48. ***Learn to delegate responsibility to capable others.***

*49. Don't forget to take a ***lunch break***. Try to get away from your desk or work are in body and mind, eve if is just 15 to 20 minutes.

*50. Forget about counting to ***10***. Count to ***1,000*** before doing something or saying anything that could make matters worse.

*51. ***Have a forgiving of events and people.*** Accept the fact that we live in an imperfect world.

*52. ***Have an optimistic view of the world.*** Believe that most people are doing the best they can.

In closing this ***52 Proven Stress Reducers***, will help you make it to the ***Super Star Winner's Circle***. The first time might be a challenge, while the second and the third and so on times will be an obsession to ***win***! These reducers through they years to come will help design a momentum to your success.

The ***Portable Cellular phone*** has become an important business tool for many "***Super Star Professionals***." To avoid being rude, users should learn to use them not only ***effectively, but appropriately***. Here are some guidelines for cellular courtesy:

*1. Keep you ringer volume low so as not to interrupt any nearby offices (at work) or tables (in a restaurant or at a prospects home or business).

*2. ***Moderate your voice.*** Find an area free of background noise so you don't need to raise your voice and disrupt others *3. don't take calls in the middle of a meeting with a prospect, customer or branch meetings. If you must take a call during a conference, leave the room so others can continue the discussion.

**What exactly is a Brand or Branded**? A brand is not just a _**well-known name**_, but a name that stands for something. Here's how to achieve a brand for your company's product, system or service:

*1. _**Take a Stand**_. When building a brand, ask yourself, "_**What does the brand stand for**_? You can't stand for something if you stand for everything.

*2. _**Narrow the Focus**_. If someone is the "_**real thing**_," you have to narrow your focus. The standard pest control service already had a company leader, such as **Bora-Care Termicide;** so when **Dow Elanco** entered the _**"Pest Elimination System."**_ It focused on "_**Termite Eradication**_" and became one of the leading brands with about 50% of the residential and commercial industry.

*3. _**Beware of brand inflation**_. Instead of narrowing the focus, management tends to inflate the brand to meaningless words. A producer may seemed to think its name meant it is a highly effective item to eliminate the problem. Not in the consumer eyes, however, for example, "_**Bora-Care**_" is a good preventative on the surface of timbers attached to the structure. both in the attic and as far below in the crawl spaces and basements. This product/brand may stop where visible and accessible. Dow Elanco System can monitor and eliminate them with installation of their monitoring system.

*4. _**Expand your business**_. Companies can narrow its focus, yet expand its business. Launch a second brand if your general service is stuck. It is always been a back up not just limited to the service your providing, but expanded to a new service and possibility a new treatment program.

Some company members often hear request they can't grant. How you respond to these grants can either _**make or break**_ a deal. A good way to deal with these request is the _**"We Love To . . ."**_ technique. When the customer says:

*1. "Of course, you throw in free delivery of the system with that, right?" (your answer)
    *   "We'd love to do that for you. The situation is though, we're passing along our extra service cost. That allows us to give you the low price you're getting.

    *   This is a much better response than:
    *   "**_No_**. We can't give you free delivery service.

Good behavior from team members needs to be reinforced with "**_Positive Praise and Positive People feedback_**". Team members repeat positive behavior among themselves, more often if it's recognized. Here's how to bring out the **_positive_** within yourselves as a team:

*1.   Keep track of whom you praise, and why. Make an effort to praise each other regularly. Keep track of the feedback you offer you can be sure you're not overlooking a fellow team member.
*2.   Encourage praise among each other at morning meetings. When team members give positive feedback to other members in the company office, morale and productivity can be boosted.
*3.   **_Keep customer in mind._** Explain to the team members how the customer benefited. This demonstrates how helping customers is also positive for the team.
*4.   Remember that teams respond differently. Some team members, especially the shy ones, feel unconfortable or embarrassed by public praise. Be **_sensitive and praise_** them in private.

The benefit of hiring a creative Super Star, to some prospects may create the same solution that **_Thomas Edison_** once did. Thomas Edison once used a test to hire a **_creative engineers_** by giving the applicant a "**_light bulb_**" and ask: "**_How much water will it hold_**?" There are **_two solutions_**:

*1.   The first applicants measured the angles of the bulb and calculated the surface area. This took up to **_20 minutes_**.
*2.   The second filled the bulb with water and poured the contents into a measuring cup. This took approximately **_one minute_**.

Engineers who chose the first solution and performed their measurements by the book were thanks politely for their time and sent on their way. The engineers who chose the second route heard Edison say, "**_Your hired_**!" Grant you that the prospects are not going to ask you the same about a product that requires a treatment tank, nor anything that might need measurements, but by using a little creativity, a **_Super Star_** could still be a **_winner_**.

Sooner or later, you may have to deal with an untrue or negative remark about company's product or service line. How you handle the situation can **make or break** the sale. It's difficult to disagree with the prospects without alienating them. Obviously, you can't say, **_"That's a lie,"_** or **_"I resent that!"_** You can, however, try to uncover the source of the misunderstanding. Do the following:

*1. **First,** assume the statement has some merit. Then probe to learn more. Say something like;

   *   **_"That's interesting. What makes you say that?" or
         I've never heard anybody say that before. Could
         you elaborate?"_**

*2. Now you can find out where your customer came up with the misconception. Their explanation can help you avoid future misunderstandings and correct the current situation immediately. Instead of being defensive, explore the criticism to find the source of the problem.

Plan each day for **_Optimum Sales Efficiency_**. What you achieve in you career is a direct result of what you accomplished each day. Here is a list of **strategies** to help you reach your **_daily goals_**:

*1. **_Plan your work day the night before_**. Before leaving the office, or your last appointment at night, make a list of activities you want to work on the next day. Rank them according to priority.

*2. **_Preview the day ahead_**. As you commute to work in the morning, run through the day's activities in your mind. Use a small tape recorder for your plan of action.

*3. **_Set aside "quiet time_**." Set aside a portion of your day to **_think, create, and plan_**. Make an appointment with yourself to avoid interruptions.

*4. **_Keep impeccable files_**. Maintain detailed files for each customer and prospect. Being able to call up exactly the facts you need to your key aspect of your effectiveness.

*5. **_Strive to improve_**. Keep a log of how you spend your time for one week. Look for areas you can improve upon—misplaced priorities, recurring time wasters, and patterns of low productivity you were aware of.

In closing this chapter, consider the quote from the writer / speaker _**Jack Falvey**_, on the _**Importance of a Good Salesperson:**_

*   "_In the age of instant price comparisons, there are no commodity items. Each product or service is attached to a unique salesperson. That person is the value added that commands a premium price, no matter what the market. Huge price differentials can't be overcome, but substantial differences surprisingly are tolerated in the interest of continued superior service and quaranteed quality._"

From the "_**Reports From The Field,**_" Sales and Marketing Management, Bill communications, New York, N.Y. 9/94

CHAPTER 14

ETHICS

Ethics, Greek ***ethika,*** from ***ethos,*** ***"character,"*** ***"custom,"*** principles or standards of human conduct, sometimes called ***morals*** (Latin ***mores,*** ***"Customs"***), and, by extension, the study of such principles, sometimes called ***moral philosophy***. For the ***Super Star Teams*** is concerned with ethics chiefly in the latter sense and is confined to that of ***Western Civilization of our industries.*** Although every culture and business has develop an ethic of its' own.

Ethics, as a branch of philosophy, is considered a ***normative*** science, because it is concerned with norms of human conduct, as distinguished from the ***formal*** sciences, such as mathematics and logic, and the ***empirical*** sciences, such as chemistry and physics. The ***empirical social sciences,*** however, including psychology, impinge to some extent on the concerns of ethics in that they study social behavior and to investigate the cultural conditions that contribute to the formation of such principles.

Ethical Principles which involve philosophers, have attempted to determine goodness in conduct according to chief principles, and have considered certain types of conduct to a particular moral standard. The former implies a final value, or ***summum bonum***, which is desirable in itself and not merely as a means to an end. In the history of ethics, some companies has stood behind with three principles of ***conduct***. Each of which has been proposed as the *(1) ***Highest Good;*** *(2) ***Happiness or Pleasure;*** *(3) ***Duty, Virtue, Obligation and Perfection,*** the fullest harmonious development of human potential.

Depending on the social setting, the authority invoked for good conduct is the will of a deity, the pattern of nature, or the rule of reason. When the will of deity is the ***authority, obedience,*** to the ***divine commandments*** in scriptural texts is the accepted standard of conduct. If the pattern of nature is the authority, conformity to the qualities attributed to human nature is the standard. When ***reason rules, behavior*** is expected to result from rational thought.

Listening Skills: A Powerful Key To Successful Negotiating. Listening skills for some negotiators need to be with good listeners. Negotiators who are poor listeners miss numerous opportunities in the counterpart's words. Statistics indicate that the normal, untrained listener is likely to understand and retain about 50 percent of a conversation. This relatively poor percentage drops to an even less than impressive 25 percent retention rate 48 hours later. This means that recall of particular conversations will usually be inaccurate and incomplete.

Many communications problems in negotiations are attributable to poor listening skills. To be a good listener, you must attempt to be ***objective***. This means you must try to understand the intentions behind your counterpart's communication—and not just what to understand. With everything your counterpart tell you, you must ask yourself:

*1.   ***"Why did he tell me that ?"***
*2.   ***"What does he think my reaction should be?"***
*3.   ***"Was he being honest?"*** and so on.

The best negotiators almost always turn out to be the ***best listeners*** as well. Why does the correlation exist? Invariably, the best negotiators have been observing the communication skills, both verbal and nonverbal, of their counterparts. They have heard and noted how other negotiators effectively use word choice and sentence structure. They have also practiced listening for the vocal skills, such as the rate of ***speech, pitch, and tonal quality***.

Experts on listening suggest that we all make at least one major listening mistake each day, and for negotiators, such mistakes can be costly. It seems obvious, but studies prove that the most successful team members are those who are able to uncover more needs than their less successful colleagues. This finding is significant since team members make their living by negotiating.

Three Pitfalls of Listening: Negotiators tend to run into three pitfalls that hinder effective listening.

*1.   Many think that negotiating is primary a job of persuasion, and to them persuasion means talking. These team members see talking as an active role and listening as a passive role. Team members tend to forget that the difficult to persuade others customers and prospects when you don't know what motivates these people.

*2. Team Member to over-prepare for what they are going to say and to use their listening time waiting for their next turn to speak. While anticipating their next change, team members may miss vital information you could use later in the negotiations.

*3. We all have emotional filters or binders that prevent us from hearing from what we don't is to hear. In my early **_Super Star_** career years, I seemed to always wasted time with the prospects who I thought would buy my service from but never did. What experience's shown me that the prospects and customers who used to waste my time had no intention of using my services. If I had been a good listener, I would have been able to pick up on their true feelings.

Attentive Listening Skills are great listening skills that dose not come easily. It is hard work. There are **_two major types_** of listening skills: **_Attentive and Interactive_**. The following **_attentive skills_** will help you better receive the **_true meanings_** your counterparts are trying to convey.

*1. **_Be motivative to listen_**. When you know that the person with the most information usually receives the better outcome in a negotiation, you have an incentive to be a better listener. It is wise to **_set goals_** for all different kinds of information you would like to receive from the counterpart. The more you can learn, the better you will be. The real challenge comes when you need to motivate yourself to listen to someone you do not like.

*2. **_If you must speak, ask questions_**. The goal is to get more specific and better refined information. To do so, you will have to continue questioning your counterpart. Your questioning sequence will be moving from the broad to the narrow, and eventually you will have the information to make the best decision. The second reason to continue asking questions is that it will help you uncover your counterpart's **_needs and wants._**

*3. **_Be alert to nonverbal cues_**. Although it is critical to listen to what is being said, it is equally important to understand the **_attitudes and motives_** behind the words. Remember, a negotiator doesn't usually put or her entire message into words. While the prospect's verbal message may convey ***honesty and convictions***, the prospect or customer ***gestures, facial, expressions, and tome of voice*** may convey doubt.

*4. ***Let your counterpart tell his or her story first***. Many team members have learned the value of this advise from the ***"School of Hard Knocks."*** Many of team members have tried to impress a new prospect by saying your company specialized in more than ***two styles of services for the prospects and customers home and businesses***. The prospect or customer then told team member that she would not be doing business with this team member's company, because their business had a need for usually one style of service. The team member replied that their company obviously did have a ***one style of service***, but the prospect or customer speaks first, he would have been able to tailor his presentation to satisfy their needs and wants.

*5. ***Do not interrupt when your counterpart is speaking***. Interrupting a speaker is not good business for two reasons.

   *1. ***It is rude.***
   *2. ***You maybe cutting off information*** that will help you as a later point in the negotiations.

Even if your counterpart is saying something that is inaccurate; ***let them finish***. If you really listen, you should gain valuable information to serve as the basis of your next question.

*6. ***Fight off distractions***. When you are negotiating, try to create a situation in which you can think clearly and avoid interruptions. ***Interruptions and distractions*** tend to prevent negotiations from proceeding smoothly or may cause a setback.

Team members, peers, children, animals, and phone can all distract you and force your eyes off your goal. If you can, create a good listening environment.

*7. ***Don't trust your memory. Write everything down***. Anytime someone tells you something in a negotiation, ***write it down*** It is amazing how much conflicting information will come up at a later time. If you are able to correct your counterpart or refresh their memory with ***facts and figures*** shared with you in an earlier session, you will earn a tremendous amount of ***credibility and power*** Writing things down may take a few minutes longer, but the results are well worth the time.

*8. ***Listen with a goal in mind***. If you have a listening goal, you can look for ***words and nonverbal cues*** that information you're seeking. When you hear specific bits of information, such as your ***counterpart's willingness to concede on the price***, you can expand with more specific questions.

*9   ***Give your counterpart your undivided attention***. It is important to look your counterpart in the eyes when they're speaking. Your goal is to create a ***win/win*** outcome so that your counterpart will be willing to negotiate with you again.

Your counterpart needs to think you are ***fair, honest, and a decent person***. One way to achieve this goal is to pay close close attention to your counterpart. Remember, look into the person eyes when their speaking. ***What message are the eyes sending? What message is their nonverbal behavior sending?*** Many experienced negotiators have found that with careful attention they can tell what their counterpart is really thinking and feeling. ***Are they lying or telling the truth?***

Are the team members nervous and desperate to complete the negotiations? Careful attention and observation will help you determine your counterpart's true meaning.

*10. ***React to the message, not to the person***. As mentioned earlier, you want your counterpart to be willing to negotiate with you again. This won't if you react to the prospect and offend his or her dignity. It is helpful to try and understand why your counterpart says the things he or she does. It is said by psychologist that "***People do what they think they have to do in order to get what they want***." This is true with negotiators.

When we negotiate, we are trying to exchange a relationship. Your counterpart is trying to change it according to their interest. If you were in your counterpart's shoes, you may do the same thing. If you are going to react, attack the message and not your counterpart personally.

*11. ***Don't get angry***. When you become angry, your counterpart has gained control in triggering your response. In the angry mode, you are probably not in the best frame of mind to make the best decisions. Emotions of any kind hinder the listening process. Anger especially interferes with the problem-solving process involved in negotiations. When you're angry, you tend to shut out your counterpart. If you're going to get angry, do it for effect, but retain control of your emotions so you can keep control of the negotiations. You may have remembered when "***Nikita Khrushchev*** pounded his shoe on the table in the United Nations? The effect worked well for him but could leave an odor with the counterpart.

*12. ***Remember, it is impossible to listen and speak at the same time***. If you are speaking, you are tipping your hand and not getting information you need from your counterpart who can help meet your needs and goals. It is more important for you to learn your counterpart's frame of reference. With the information of your counterpart, you will be in control of the negotiations. When you are in control, you will be ***acting*** and your counterpart will be ***reacting***. It is usually better to be the one in the ***driver's seat.***

Interactive Listening Skills: The second type of listening skills are those used to ***interact with the speaker***. These skills help ensure that you understand what the sender is communicating, and they acknowledge the sender's feelings. ***Interactive Skills Include***: [a] ***Clarifying*** [b] ***Verifying*** [c] ***Reflecting***.

*   ***Clarifying*** is using facultative questions to clarify information, get additional information, and explore all sides of an issue. ***Examples: "Can you clarify this***?" "***What specific information do you want?***" "***When do want the inspection report?***"
*   ***Verifying*** is paraphrasing the speaker's words to ensure understanding and to check the meaning and the interpretation with them. ***Examples: "As I understand it, your plan is*** . . ." "***It sounds like you're saying*** . . ." "***This is what you've decided and the reasons are*** . . ."
*   ***Reflecting*** is making empathetic remarks that acknowledge the speaker's feelings. If negotiators are to create ***win/win*** outcomes, they must be empathetic. Most team members think themselves as ***relatively empathetic***. In fact, most of us easily feel empathy for others who are experiencing what we have experienced. But true

empathy is a _**skill**_ not a _**memory**_. Negotiators who have developed the ability to emphasize can display it even when encountering counterparts with whom they have little in common. The ability of a negotiator to emphasize has been found to significantly affect the counterpart's behavior and attitudes.

**To be Empathetic**, negotiators need to accurately perceive the content of the message.

* They need to give attention to the emotional components and the unexpressed core meanings of the message.
* The need to attend to the feelings of the other, but remain detached, whereas a _**sympathetic individual**_ would adopt those feelings as their own. _**Empathy**_ involves understanding and relating to another's feelings. _**Examples: "I can see that you were frustrated because . . ." "You felt that you didn't get a fair shake." "You seem very confident that you can do a great job for . . ."**_

**To truly practice reflective listening**, you must make no judgments and pass along no opinions or provide and solutions. You simply acknowledge the sender's emotional content. _**Examples: Sender: "How do you expect me to complete the project by next Monday**_?"

**Reflective Response: It sounds like you are overwhelmed by your increased workload**.

**Or Sender: "Hey Mary, what's the idea of not approving my requisition for another project ?"**

**Reflective Response: "You sound really over not getting your request approved."**

If your _**reflective response**_ is constructed properly, the natural reaction from your counterpart will be provide more explanation and information. Here are some keys points you will find helpful in learning to be _**empathetic**_.

*1. _**Recognize and Identify Emotions**_. Most experienced negotiators are not adept at recognizing the _**myriad**_ (unidentified) _**emotions**_. You will find it easier to identify other's emotions if you can easily identify your own. Are you _**frustrated, stressed, angry, happy, sad, or nervous**_.

*2. **_Rephrase the Content._** If you restate your counterpart's comments word for word, they'll be willing to believe you are parroting them. doing so, not only sounds awkward, but will make your counterpart angry. The key is to restate the content using different words.

*3. **_Make Noncommittal Responces_**. A good way to start reflective statements is with such phrases as "**_It sounds Like_**," "**_It appears that . . . ,_**" "**_It seems like_** . . . ." These phrase work well because they are **_noncommittal_**. If you blatantly state, "**_You are angry because_** . . . ." most people will proceed to tell you why you are incorrect.

*4. **_Make Educated Guesses_**. When involved in an negotiation in which one negotiator told the counterpart that the other had submitted a ridiculous offer in an attempt to get you to buy a service. The negotiator responded, "**_It almost sounds like you are insulted by the offer?_**" The counterpart may reply, "**_Not insulted, just shock_**." Although the negotiator was not entirely accurate in his assessment of his counterpart's emotion of a good quality service, it was a good educated guess.

Remember, when you want to improve your **_listening skills_**, a a good rule to remember is that **_God_** gave us **_two ears and one mouth_**. You should use them in their respective active proportions. To succeed in negotiations, you must understand the **_needs, wants, and motivations_** of your counterpart. To understand those **_needs, you must hear_**. To **_hear, you must listen_** . . . . Remember not to be a **_Dumbbell_**, by breaking out of the **_self-destructive cycles_**.

*1. **_Learn how to listen to criticism._**
*2. **_Learn how to deal with others._**
*3. **_Learn to admit a need for help._**

There is an old saying by **_Teddy Roosevelt, President,_** "**_Find the person who is about to screw up your life. Learn what you need to learn from that person, and do what has to be done to prevent that person from destroying your career . . . That person, of course, is yourself._**"

President Roosevelt also had ___Seven Steps to Setting More Attainable Goals:___

*1. *Decide exactly what you want to accomplish and why*. Don't use vague terms.
*2. *Do your homework*. Get the facts you need. Find out everything you need to reach your goals realistic.
*3. *Set up a plan of action*. Develop a step-step path that you will follow to reach your goals. Break down larger task into smaller ones.
*4. *Set a timetable.* Be realistic, but not ___lackadaisical.___ Your timetable show allow you enough time to accomplished each step, but not so much time that you become unmotivated. ___Challenge Yourself___.
*5. *Do it.* Nothing happens until you take the first step. You've devised your plan, now take the plunge.
*6. *Make constant reevaluations.* Review your progress on a weekly or monthly basis. Be flexible; don't be afraid to change your plan if things aren't going like you envisioned they would.
*7. ___Keep Going___. Nobody said it was going to be easy. The difference between the ___top five percent___ of an profession and the rest is that extra effort required to get back up again and move ahead when everyone else has given up.

CHAPTER 15

LEARNING LEADERSHIP

It is widely known that promoting team members with technical knowledge and skills has failed to provide the leadership to some modern organizations. The best specialist are not automatically endowed with team leader skills. This widely-known leadership deficit highlight significant inadequacies for traditional training solutions.

Where and how team leaders develop the leadership? In a strait but brief terms:

*1. Leadership development is successful when leadership behaviors change.
*2. Senior team leaders "***knowing things***" or "***being able to do things***" is not enough.
*3. Developing leaders need to choose to change how they behave.
*4. Telling leaders to change doesn't work as much as insincerity in relationships doesn't work.

Successful team leaders make very powerful and personal choices about how they relate with themselves and their followers. These ***team leader-follower relationships*** are more than just ***work relationships***. Great team leaders know the social value of companies are larger than you can measure. Larger cultural trends are automatically changing companies social processes also. These social processes are immune companies structures because they are ***self-orangizing and informal***. Many more are aware of modern team leaders, who have realized larger cultural and social trends of demanding **_transformations_** at many levels for individuals. Teams and whole companies organizations as they recreate themselves with greater:

*1. Personal authenticity and collaborative individualism . . . .
*2. Organizational and personal responsibility, stewardship and autonomy . . . .
*3. Consultation and agreement-making . . .
*4. Balance of outcome and process focusing . . .
*5. Balance of business and community interest . . . .

These multi-level transformations demand more of modern team leaders than traditional learning of knowledge and skills. Company leadership often requires team leaders and members to change their image of their roles within themselves.

In leadership development terms, companies are rediscovering the distinctions between management and leadership. Leadership is the forge for the change, or envision management, as being about:

*1. Planning and organizing.
*2. Controlling and problem solving.
*3. Focusing on outcomes.

And "*Leadership,*" as being about:

*1. Creating a vision and developing strategies.
*2. Enrolling, motivating and inspiring people.
*3. Building trust and having courage.
*4. Creating action . . . .

Traditional Management Development offers a seductive and easy **_short-term_** success but it is not achieving leadership and emotional human complexity. **_Leadership Skills Development_** is the term of "**_road less traveled_**" for a myriad of reasons, and not least being a central realization that it is a **_never-ending journey_** with no tidy right or wrong "**_answers_**." Awareness of the need for a balance of both technical (rational) and soft (extra-rational) skills in leadership is, at one level, is now so old many of us have grown to tolerate the imbalance.

In some cases of designing and facilitating leadership development programs, there are some "***would-be-leaders*** obstacles . . . . These obstacles are the:

    *1.   Leaning helplessness and the belief of:
        *a.   *"I can't make a difference."*
        *b.   *"They won't let me make a difference."*

    *2.   A need to heal the past and relieve resentment for leaders previously inhumane and unsuccessful actions.
    *3.   Paralyzing fear of retribution based upon unchallenged company mythology.
    *4.   Low Self **Awareness**, emotional maturity and responsibility. These are often evident in chronically poor social skills, relationship skills, and the habitual blaming of others for team and organizational ills.

The following list is by no means exhaustive and yet it show the common theme of "***Extra-Rational Obstacles***:"
The issues of:

    *1.   ***Self-Image***
    *2.   ***Learned helplessness***
    *3.   ***Fear and Emotional Responsibility*** . . .
         are essentially extra-rational and require suitably extra-rational development solutions. Knowing leadership theory and having leadership micro skills does not "***make***" a leader. Candidates often satisfy perfectly rational leadership competencies and still fail to lead. Traditional information-based and cognitive training often don't deliver behavioral change with regard to leadership . . . .

An example of an "***Extra-Rational Process***," requiring ***Extra-Rational and Experimental learning*** is the action of blindly touching your nose . . . .

    *1.   Reach out in front of your face with one hand.
    *2.   Close your eyes and gently touch your nose.
    *3.   Now think about how you learned to complete this simple task.

The action is simple and you can learned it from many repeated events over time. The ***Micro Muscle Movement*** **and** ***Special Awareness*** can be complex and you now unconsciously process vast amount of information to complete this task.

Now, imagine how hard it would be to learn to blindly touching your nose from the information rather from the experience. This extra-rational process of blindly touching your nose, like leadership, is the best learned experience. Research has shown that some subjects are also attributing portions of their leadership learning and development to traditional training. This leading relationship of elements are best defined by four approaches to leadership development:

*1. Conceptional theories
*2. Micro skill-building
*3. Personal growth and self-awareness
*4. Feedback and learning about yourself from others.

In conclusion, leadership development is not a totally rational process . . . . Traditional information or competency training need to be enhanced by:

*1. Extra-rational
*2. Experimental and
*3. Personal development process.

No matter how much your company crave simple, quantifiable solutions to satisfy the tail-end of the economic rationalist management fad, simple, rational solutions don't exist. When you invest in the leadership development, this will not just teach team members, but will teach:

*1. Information
*2. Knowledge
*3. Training technical skills.

Learning leadership is far more difficult, personal and extra-rational. our investments may surprise your company and team members.

Leadership and Team Membership is turning complaining customers into sales by:

*1. <u>**Making Adjustments**</u>: After the customer has calm down, offer to make it up to them in the best possible way. Repair or replace the item, adjust the service, or rectify previous rude behavior with the understanding. Always give a little than the customer expects . . .

*2. <u>**Now Keep On Selling**</u>**!** Handling complaints well established your credibility. You've put the customer in the better mood and they trust you. Now is a good time to introduce them to additional products and services.

*3. <u>**Taking steps towards helping complaining customers means you're on the path towards increase in sales**</u> . . .

When tackling the difficult projects, you as the leader or team member has <u>***nine steps***</u> on how to tackle them:

*1. ***Don't delay too long.***
*2. ***Pinpoint the worst parts or points of the task.***
*3. ***Break the entire assignment into parts.***
*4. ***Schedule the assignment.***
*5. ***hysically organize the task.***
*6. ***Don't get hung up on the trivial facets of your task.***
*7. ***Visualize the completion of the project.***
*8. ***Make it a game.***
*9. ***Seek advice, talk it out.***

Written business proposals are in an accepted and growing way to obtain new businesses. This can be a painful problem for a small growing businesses team members. Some are accustomed to dealing only through quotations and personal contact.

<u>**Proposals**</u> are the long hallmark of giant companies. They have become the preferred method of selecting the best and concluding new business contracts. Primitive proposal forms of proposals maybe required by local offices for local residential homes, school districts and city councils, yet require the "<u>**Full-fledged**</u> proposals becoming the rule, rather than the exceptional.

Although writing and preparing a proposal may not be easy, nor instinctive based on your previous business methods, proposal preparation and delivery techniques can be learned and used by you. The results are favorable, because proposals open up a new avenues of business or, perhaps, keep up with a trend traditional business practices are now taking.

But what is a proposal? Proposals are different and distinctive from just about any other form of business you can imagine. Different from:

*1. _**Advertising**_
*2. _**Promotion**_
*3. _**Description of products and services**_.

In a nutshell, a proposal is a presentation which answers a need stated by a _**Request for Proposal**_, (or better known as **R.F.P.**) issued by the procuring customer.

The proposal responds in many ways, to all the requirements cited in the "_**Request for Proposal.**_" Your proposals rated against similar proposals submitted by the other hopeful companies. The winning contractor is selected based upon the evaluator's reading of the proposal:

*1. *The Quality*
*2. *The Content and*
*3. *The Scope of your Proposals.*

There is also something called the _**Unsolicited Proposal**_, which is submitted because of a suspected need for the services your company offers. This proposal is not competitive and is not a response to a **R.F.P.** This proposal is not competitive and is not a response to an **R.F.P.** An unsolicited proposal must first:

*1. Convince the customer that there is a problem and you have the solution. *Or*
*2. The need that your products and services address.

There is also a known proposal method, known as the "_**Sole-Source Proposal**_, in which you bid by yourself for a new or (usually) follow-on work. There may have been an **R.F.P.,** but "_**new**_," you are requested to complete additional work. You are required to submit a proposal for the additional work. Although you may not lose the job to somebody else, you may not get the additional work if the proposal does not live up to the expectations regarding:

*1. *Quality*
*2. *Presentation*
*3. *Price!*

Proposals are requested to protect the procurer from criticism involving favoritism or an otherwise unsound selection of contractors. Unfortunately, this concern has become more prevalent in an increasingly litigious society. In addition, the specifications are more complete from a sufficient field of willing and competent bidders. There is always the risk that the contract will never be issued because of the expense and the time factors, or perhaps the project is not "***cost-effective***."

The trouble with proposals is the discipline required to follow the **R.F.P.** to the letter. An **R.F.P.** is the product of the procuring the customer who has the interest in you or your company as a paramount. What the customer wants is important than what you want to sell. The way in which they want it may be just as important. The cost of the product or services is usually much more important than *quality*.

Instructions for the proposal preparation is that part of the **R.F.P.** which tells you to stay at a minimum, and the order in which to say it, maybe vague and disjointed. Careful study and advance knowledge of the procurer's business needs will help reduce the double meaning and allow for a better proposal. Only respond to what you are asked. Offering more may make you less competitive than other bidders who conformed to their proposal to the **R.F.P.** and provide answers to the questions asked. Usually, there is a short time span between the receipt of the **R.F.P.** and the submission of the deadline. The time and effort that goes into the preparation and submission of a proposal can be very costly. Accept the reality that proposals have to be prepared if your company will continue to grow.

Overcoming your lack of experience, insight and resources to do a credible job and increase your chances of getting the contract.

Assess your business assets and resources to determine what proposals you can submit from the demands of the contract, and therefore, could make on your operations.

In summary, mastering the art of proposal and leadership is a must for individuals and territorial team members. Proposals can be costly and there are no guarantees that a bid will be accepted. Exert diligent effort in the right direction . . . .

For the next ten plus pages are samples of a proposal package. Review all of it, and determine what is going to take for you set out to do the same . . . .

Customize Proposal Package

For:

{Company Name}

Add a sentence or two describing the specific project

You and Company's Name
Address Line 1
Address Line 2
City, State, Province Postal Code
Phone Number
Fax Number
Date

Title of Proposal

Table of Contents

BACKGROUND:

Answer the question: **"Why are you writing this proposal?"** Explain who wants the projects and why. List details leading up to the proposal.

*1. It it a follow up to a meeting? If so, jog your readers' memories by explaining who was at the meeting and what was discussed.
*2. It is cold solicitation, based on an idea you have? If so, make your background compelling to the reader. Otherwise, you'll lose them within the first page.
*3. Were you asked to make a proposal via a Request for Proposal? If so, make sure you refer to the request here.

EXECUTIVE SUMMARY:

Provide a brief summary of the key points you'll address in detail in the proposal.

*1. Write a brief statement of the problems, needs, and solutions or recommendations as you see them.
*2. Grab attention of your audience by knowing their concerns and addressing each one.
*3. Briefly describe the objectives of your proposal, and your plans to meet those objectives.
*4. Make it clear how your plan will benefit their organization.
*5. Explain how you'll evaluate your plan. How will you measure whether or not you've succeeded?

INTRODUCTION:

Strongly motivate your audience to continue reading the proposal. Again, grab their attention by knowing exactly what their concerns are. Establish who you are, where your expertise lies, and why you're the one who can do the best job.

Establish your capabilities to do the job. If you've completed similar projects before, say so, and invite the reader to contact other firms you've worked with. However, do not go into details. Refer the reader to where they can find details later in the proposal.

*   **Statement of Problems/Need**

*1. State why you are submitting this proposal. What need or problem are you addressing?
*2. Demonstrate a clear understanding of the organization's problems/ needs.

*   **Project Scope and Objectives**

Provide general information concerning staffing and time frame for completing the work; when work will begin, how it will take to complete.

*1. How many people will be working on the project?
*2. How long with the project take?
*3. Will the project require one team, or several teams of specialist?
*4. What are the objectives of each team or person? Link each objective to a detailed result, not to an activity (don't explain how or why something will be done; these questions will be answered later).

ACTION PLAN:

Argue the strengths and weakness of possible approaches. Describe your approach, and your reason for choosing your company.

*1. Describe project activities in detail and show how they satisfy your objectives.
*2. If your plan is unique, explain how, and show why unique means better.

* **Activity One**
    * Describe how you will meet your first objective. Include any tables, charts, graphs, statistics, etc. that help describe the work you'll be doing.

* **Activity Two**
    * Describe how you'll meet your second objective. Include tables, charts, graphs, statistics, etc. that help describe the work you'll be doing.

* **Activity Three**
    * Describe how you'll meet your third objective. Include tables, charts, graphs, statistics, etc. that help describe the work you'll be doing.

MANAGEMENT PLAN

*   Describe your approach to managing the project.

*   **Project Organization**
        *   Show who is responsible for each stage of the project. If it's a large project, you might include an organizational chart.

*   **Costs**
        *   Provide the high level labor and material costs of the project. Include detailed labor and material costs in the appendices.

*   **Schedule**
        *   Provide a high level schedule showing start dates, finish dates, and contacts for key project milestones. Include a detailed project schedule in the Appendices.

RESULTS

* Describe with a reduce size copy of the Inspection Report on the findings and recommendations. Focus on the benefits you will pass on to the customer.

EVALUATION

* Here you need to describe how you'll measure the extent to which you've met the objectives, and the extent to which the results are consistent with your plan.

QUALIFICATIONS

* Summarize your company's resources, accomplishments, and abilities. Prove that you're as well as capable. In the Appendices, refer the reader to the copies of the documentation you choose to provide.

CONCLUSIONS/NEXT STEPS

*   Explain what happens next. How soon do you plan to contact the client/customer to discuss the proposal? Do you want to set up a meeting to discuss it?

APPENDICES

*   The following are some suggestions for this section:
    * **1.**   Letters of references
    * **2.**   Letters of endorsement, certifications
    * **3.**   Resumes of key staff members
    * **4.**   Award earned by the company/organization
    * **5.**   Sub-contractor information
    * **6.**   Project company/Organization, Staffing
    * **7.**   Schedules
    * **8.**   Costs
    * **9.**   Proposal Terms and Conditions
    * **10.** Additional information, such as drawings, figures, tables, slides, charts, statistics
    * **11.** Supplemental information of interest to only a few readers
    * **12.** Definitions of Terms

In conclusion to this chapter and the book, knowing your audience are the guidelines for writing the proposal. Learn as much about your audience as you can. Before writing the proposal gather some accurate information about their goals and needs. Do library research. Check for articles about the clients organization and company in professional journals, magazines and newspapers before entering into a business transaction. As a leader, learn about their products and or services. Talk with employees, supervisors, and key executive of the company and organization.

Understand and respond to your reader's needs as well as the organization needs. Contact and write the proposal from the point of view of your customer. You must know their expectations and they may respond to their unique needs. Tell them what you can do to help reach their goals for the service or what the product will perform. Always show them why your plan is the best and compare your plan with your competitors.

The proposal should be tailored to your audience needs. Remember to find out their kind of personality the company or organization has. Determine who will be reading the proposal and what information and style they'll expect. Be consistent, because once you on their style, whether informal to formal, write each section to match their style.

Never forget your competitors and most of all do some research on them. Determine what they're doing and whether their maybe better. Always Provide products and services that your competitors can't. Show the comparison to the reader if request. Get their attention. Create a high quality professional-looking proposal. Not a hand written one with your business card. This is the first product you'll deliver to a customer or client, so you want to make it a good one. Emphasize that this product and service is important to your and their business. Show them high priority. Provide compelling introductions and headings. Emphasize the importance of certain parts of the proposal. Always encourage the reader to act on the proposal by proving that doing so, will be in the right direction toward any positive changes.

Evaluate your proposal with leadership. Review your proposal, and ask your team members who aren't involved with the project under your leadership.

Under your leadership, is your writing clear, compelling, and Motivating to the point? Will it be easy to read? Your visual aids within your proposal, do they describe the project in detail? Make sure that the activities are well thought out, and not too fuzzy, ambiguous or too general. Paragraphs and sentences need to be short and easy to read, so that the reader does n't ask too many questions.

Avoid clichés within the proposal. Chose the objectives carefully and used them sparingly. Avoid or limit your professional or technical terms or jargon and acronyms. Did you used an active rather than passive speech? (i.e. "We will complete your service by . . . ." rather than "The service will be completed by . . . .")

Within your writing, be straight forward, and make the reading to the reader enjoyable. As a team member or the leader, your style writing should be consistent throughout the proposal package. Make sure that the writing is free from grammatical mistakes. Remember to adequately defined all the terms you used. Each section in details is important, so avoid any fluffy sentences within the proposal.

Finally, the logical flow of ideas and a sense of continuity throughout your proposal and career, will always improve the impact of your service, products, proposal and your future career. Always remember that "Leadership and Team Membership," should "***Adapt, Improvise, and Overcome the Objectives.***

That is your motive to be successful with one company veers several companies at a time of your life . . . .